Books by Kenneth E. Long

Trump's Economic Era

Economic Essentials - Theory and Application

And They will Riot in the Streets
 - A Nation Deceived is a Nation Enslaved

Personal Finance
- Beware of Wolves in Sheep's Clothing

Introduction to Economics

The Great Economic Debate

AUSTRIANS vs KEYNESIANS

By Kenneth E. Long

Rose of Sharon Publishers

Rose of Sharon Publishers

RoseofSharonPublishers@gmail.com

Cover design by
Photo by Brotin Biswas from Pexels

ISBN 13: 978-0-9963327-2-9 (print)
ISBN 13: 978-0-9963327-3-6 (ebook)

ACKNOWLEDGMENT

I am indebted to my wife Kay, who has painstakingly edited the manuscript, and Steven Macon, whose knowledge of the publishing business was invaluable.

INTRODUCTION

Austrians believe in free markets where sustainable growth depends on clear price signals. Keynesians support an interventionist public sector, generous wealth redistribution policies, and deficit spending to maintain full employment. Whereas Austrians emphasize supply-side economics, Keynesians believe that we can manage the economy if we can manage demand. Austrians believe that slumps are inevitable, and we hinder prosperity when we do not let this natural process run its course. Keynesians believe that the government can alleviate slumps with the appropriate fiscal policies. Politicians mostly favor Keynesian policies.

Austrians recognize the implications of Goodhart's Law. Named after British economist Charles Goodhart, Goodhart explained the law in a 1975 article on monetary policy. The law states that "when a measure becomes a target, it ceases to be a good measure." According to Goodhart's Law, when Keynesians set targets for full employment, inflation, and interest rates, we end up with dishonest markets. The manipulation of markets leads to false price signals, and without valid price signals, we no longer have free markets. Austrians believe that the government sabotages the economy when it subsidizes too much, taxes too much, and regulates too much.

CONTENTS

Economist Norm Franz once stated:

"Gold is the money of kings, silver is the money of gentlemen, barter is the money of peasants—but debt is the money of slaves."

TERMS AND CONCEPTS

SCARCITY

Scarcity does not mean rare; scarcity means that there are not enough goods (something tangible) or services (something intangible) to meet consumers' wants and needs at a zero price. In a free market, the price mechanism decides who gets what and how much. A free good or service is a good or service whereby there is plenty for everyone who wants it at a zero price. Water from a public drinking fountain is an example of a free good.

THE ECONOMIC PROBLEM

The economic problem is that there is always scarcity, and resources are insufficient to satisfy our wants and needs. Therefore, we have to determine what to produce and how best to allocate land, labor, capital, and entrepreneurship. Economics studies this fundamental economic problem.

Macro means large; macroeconomics examines the economy in the large, such as unemployment, national income, rate of growth, gross domestic product, inflation, and price levels. Macroeconomics focuses on the movement and trends in the economy as a whole. Micro means small; microeconomics focuses on the decision making process by people and firms. How do we make decisions to maximize our welfare? How does a business

1

choose the best price and the best quantity to produce to maximize their profits or minimize their losses?

ECONOMICS IS A THOUGHT PROCESS

More than anything else, economics is a thought process of cause and effect. The following terms and principles will help your thought process.

Opportunity Cost

Economics forces us to make choices, and every decision entails an opportunity cost. Opportunity cost is that which you give up in the best alternative when making a decision. For example, when you attend a lecture—how much money are you giving up? If you could make ten dollars an hour and you have three hours vested in the lecture, your opportunity cost is thirty dollars. Opportunity cost can be a pleasure you are giving up in the best choice. What would you rather be doing if you were not class? If you are giving up the joy of fishing, then that foregone pleasure is an opportunity cost. On a macro scale we must make decisions, and every decision entails an opportunity cost.

Marginal Analysis

You use marginal analysis each time you make a decision. The term margin means the last unit or the previous increment. Marginal benefit is the benefit from your last action, and marginal cost is the cost of that last act. For example, imagine standing in front of a soda machine. How many dollar sodas will you purchase? To answer this question, economists always start with the first soda. Will you or will you not buy the first soda? You will buy the first soda if your marginal benefit is greater than your marginal cost. In other words, if you value the soda more than you value a dollar, you will exchange a dollar for a soda. Will you purchase a second soda? The answer is the same, yes, if you value the second soda more than you value a dollar. You will not buy a third soda if your marginal benefit is less than your marginal cost. Each time you make a decision, you go through this same thought process.

Leverage

Suppose you need to move a thousand-pound rock, what would you do? You would place a smaller rock next to it and put a long pole on the small rock and under the big rock. The longer the bar, the easier it will be to move the big rock. In so doing, you are using the pole as leverage to move the rock. Some people use borrowed money as leverage to buy stock, which economists call purchasing stock on the margin. You can buy, let's say, $1,000 worth of stock by investing $500 of your own money and borrowing the rest from your stockbroker. However, when the stock price falls, your losses are magnified. When a company has more debt than equity, economists say that it is "highly leveraged."

Price Elasticity of Demand

Price elasticity of demand is a measure of a consumer's responsiveness to a change in price. When a price change has a small effect on the quantity demanded, demand is inelastic. If a good faces an inelastic demand curve, a price increase will increase total revenue; the money gained exceeds the money lost. The demand for a good is elastic when a price change will affect the quantity demanded. With an elastic demand curve, a price increase will reduce total revenue; money lost exceeds money gained.

Moral Hazard

A moral hazard occurs when someone pursues an activity without regard to potential losses because there is no penalty for the loss or failure. For example, a banker is willing to make risky investments because he believes the government will cover his losses. You may be careful when making decisions if you know you will bear the consequences of a wrong decision, but you will tend to take more risks if you know that someone else will pay the cost of your wrong decision.

Rent-Seeking

Rent-seeking occurs when people seek a bigger slice of the economic pie rather than make the pie bigger; rent-seekers make money without producing more goods or services. Whether legal or illegal, rent-seekers impose economic costs. The following are examples of rent-seeking:

- A gang demands protection money from a business owner.
- A union may demand higher wages without offering an increase in worker' productivity.
- Firms lobby Congress for preferential treatment.

Stock vs. Flow

What effect will a national minimum wage law have on the economy? The answer depends on your point of view. One line of reasoning supports a national wage standard because higher wages will increase consumer demand, increase production, and more jobs. This line of reasoning is looking at a national minimum wage as a stock variable. A stock variable measures something at a particular point in time. At times economists will use the terms "static" and "dynamic" instead of the words "stock" and "flow" to describe these events.

If people can earn higher wages, everything else being equal, consumer demand will increase. But can we assume that nothing else will change when the government imposes a minimum wage on the nation? What effect will this government-imposed mandate have on businesses? Will this mandate increase costs for business? And if so, what impact will these higher costs have on employment?

A flow variable is a variable over an interval of time. If variable A changes, variable B might change, which might affect C, etc. When Congress makes decisions to do this or that, there is a tendency for politicians to look at things as a stock situation and not consider the flow. For example, politicians tend to believe that a ten percent tax increase will increase government revenue by ten percent. But this approach to decision making ignores dynamic analysis. Dynamic analysis recognizes that when taxes increase by ten percent, the level of consumption and investments are affected.

Economies of Scale

Economies of scale recognize that as the scale of operation increases for a business, its costs decrease over the long run, time in which a firm can change its plant capacity. A larger size typically allows a firm to take on more specialized machines. It can take advantage of skilled labor, which contributes to lower costs as productivity increases. The increase in efficiency allows a firm to lower its price to increase its total sales. For example, a farmer who owns a small farm may not purchase an expensive modern tractor. A farmer who owns a big farm can justify buying a large, expensive tractor (more efficient) because of the large volume.

By forcing smaller competitors to raise their wages, larger firms are put in a favorable position because they can afford the high salaries due to its economies of scale. The small competitor may not afford the higher wage because of its higher costs. By driving smaller competitors out of the market, larger firms can increase their market share. Large corporations have an incentive to engage in rent-seeking in hopes of convincing politicians in Washington DC to raise the minimum wage.

Fiat Currency

Fiat money is a currency that lacks intrinsic value and is established as a legal tender by government regulation. The U.S. dollar is fiat money, as are the euro and many other major world currencies. Most of the world's money is called fiat money, meaning it is accepted as money because a government says that it's legal tender, and the public has enough confidence and faith in the money's ability to serve as a storage medium for purchasing power. On June 5, 1933, the United States went off the gold standard, a monetary system in which currency is backed by gold, when Congress enacted a joint resolution nullifying the right of creditors to demand payment in gold. The United States had been on a gold standard since 1879, except for an embargo on gold exports during World War I, but bank failures during the Great Depression of the 1930s frightened the public into hoarding gold, making the policy untenable. The government held the $35 per ounce price until August 15, 1971, when President Richard Nixon announced that the United States would no longer convert dollars to gold at a fixed value upon demand by foreign governments, thus completely abandoning the gold standard.

The Derivatives Market

Derivatives are contracts between parties; they are speculations on some future event. The value of a derivative is reliant upon or derived from an underlying asset or group of assets. In other words, the value of a derivative is derived from the value of something else. The most common underlying assets for derivatives are stocks, bonds, commodities, currencies, interest rates, and market indexes. Derivative contracts are a part of the "futures" market because the results will take place in the future. Two parties can bet on anything, such as the price of a stock, the price of an agricultural product, exchange rates on the international market, or anything else. The derivative market is the largest market in the world.

Let's say you and I make a bet that it will rain or the sun will shine on some future date, for example, May 5. We wager one hundred dollars, and we draw up a contract and both sign it. I bet that the sun will shine, and you bet that it will rain that day. If the sun shines, you own me one hundred dollars, if it rains, I owe you one hundred dollars. This contract now has a value of one hundred dollars to whomever is on the winning side of the bet. Now let's say that you want out of the contract. You can sell you're your part of the contract to someone else. They will pay you whatever the two of you agree upon.

Hedge Fund

Hedge funds are alternative investments using pooled funds that employ different strategies to earn active returns for their investors. A hedge fund is a pooled investment fund that trades in relatively liquid assets and is able to make extensive use of more complex trading, and risk management techniques in an attempt to improve performance. A liquid asset is an asset that can easily be converted into cash within a short amount of time.

Margin Call

Buying stock on the margin means that a person buys stock with borrowed money. A margin call occurs when the value of an investor's margin account falls below the broker's required amount. An investor's margin account contains securities bought with borrowed money (typically a combination of the investor's own money and money borrowed from the investor's broker). A margin call refers specifically to a broker's demand that an investor deposit additional money or securities into the account so that it is brought up to the minimum value, known as the maintenance margin. A margin call is usually an indicator that one or more of the securities held in the margin account has decreased in value. When a margin call occurs, the investor must choose to either deposit more money in the account or sell some of the assets held in their account. When Bill Hwang's hedge fund Archegos defaulted on a margin call he was forced to sell $30 billion in stock to satisfy the call.

Hegemony

Hegemony refers to the dominance by either a social group or a country over others. The dominance may either be economic, political, or military. The term originated from the Greek word "hegemon" meaning "leader" or simply "dominance over." Hegemony is the position of being the strongest and most powerful and therefore able to control others.

Federal Reserve

The Federal Reserve is America's central bank. President Woodrow Wilson, and Congress gave up control over the nation's money supply when it transferred authority from the government to the world private banking cabal with the Federal Reserve Act of 1913. A cartel of eight families owns the Federal Reserve and other central banks around the world. They are Goldman Sachs of New York, Rockefeller Brothers of New York, Rothschild Banks of London and Berlin, Lazard Brothers of Paris, Israel Moses Sieff Banks of Italy, Kuhn and Loeb and Company of Germany and New York, and the Warburg Bank of Hamburg and Amsterdam. The Federal Reserve is listed in the telephone book's white pages, while the US Treasury is listed in the yellow pages. Fed employees' email address ends in .org, not .gov.

Commercial banks can multiply money, but only central banks can create money. Before the banking system can multiply money, someone has to make a deposit. But the Federal Reserve does not need a deposit; it can create money by merely pushing a few keys on its computer to credit a client's account by X amount. All currencies are debt instruments; they are floating abstractions that profit the world's bankers. At the top of a dollar bill is printed "Federal Reserve Note." A note is an IOU; it is an agreement to pay interest to the note owner, the Federal Reserve. Dollars come into existence when the government sells bonds to the Federal Reserve, therefore it (we who pay taxes) pays interest to the bankers. The Bureau of Engraving and Printing of the government converts only a small fraction of this borrowed money into physical dollars.

Modern Monetary Theory

Modern Monetary Theory (MMT) is a big departure from conventional economic theory. It proposes governments that control their own currency can spend freely, as they can always create more money to pay off debts in their own currency. The theory suggests government spending can grow the economy to its full capacity, enrich the private sector, eliminate unemployment, and finance major programs such as universal healthcare, free college tuition, and green energy. If the spending generates a government deficit, this isn't a problem either. The government's deficit is, by definition, the money we owe to ourselves. Keynesian economists tend to support this MMT, while Austrians see it as inflationary and a ticking time bomb that will eventually destroy the economy.

Cantillon Effect

In our modern economy, the Cantillon Effect is at play with a stratified socioeconomic impact, favoring investors over wage-earners. Cantillon's original thesis outlines how rising prices affect different sectors at different times and suggests that time difference effectively acts as a taxing mechanism. Modern Monetary Theory (easy money policies) favors investors over wage earners because the monied class has preference in the loanable funds market, the market where people lend and borrow money, and wage earners get the dregs. The artificially low-interest rates favor the rich over the poor, the asset class over the wage earner. The Cantillon Effect illustrates how the uneven distribution of wealth in society grows ever more uneven with low-interest rates. The low-interest rates favor investors while the average income person receives less interest income on their savings.

Thucydides Trap

When an emerging power threatens to displace an existing power, there is a tendency toward conflict and sometimes war. When the existing power relies on its military and its political influence instead of competing economically with the rising power, the emerging power ultimately gains dominance over the current regime. A characteristic of a Thucydides Trap is when the declining power is guilty of hubris. Hubris was a character flaw often seen in the heroes of classical Greek tragedy, including Oedipus and Achilles. The familiar old saying "Pride goeth before a fall" is talking about hubris. Hubris describes a personality quality of extreme or foolish pride or dangerous overconfidence, often in combination with arrogance and the over extension of resources. When the art of diplomacy between powers declines, when the declining power relies on brute force, this indicates that we are in a Thucydides Trap.

False Flags

A false flag concocts a crisis, stirs a reaction, then proposes a solution that will convince people to support a policy that they would otherwise not support. Perpetrators of false flags are masters of deception. A false flag event will stir emotions and will be followed by a news blitz. Shortly after, authorities will identify a scapegoat with little or no concrete facts to back up the accusation. The higher the shock value, the more spectacular the event, the more people killed, or claimed killed, the more severe the unemployment and bankruptcies, the fewer people will question the authenticity of the occurrence. The term comes from the old days of wooden ships when a ship would hang the flag of its enemy before attacking one of its own—then it would blame the enemy for the attack and thereby gain public support.

Stovepiping and Gaslighting

Stovepiping is similar to false flags. Whereas a false flag uses an incident to convince people to take action, stovepiping uses incorrect information to sway public opinion. Gaslighting sows seeds of doubt in a person or a group, hoping to make them question their memory or cherished beliefs. The term "Gaslighting" comes from a 1938 play by Patrick Hamilton. Throughout the play, the abusive husband, Gregory, manipulates Paula to make her believe she has gone mad. He leads her to think she's stealing things without realizing it and hearing noises that are not there. Gaslighting hides truths from the victim—thus, the perpetrators of gaslighting seek power and control.

ESG

ESG stands for Environmental, Social, and Governance, and refers to the three key factors when measuring the sustainability and ethical impact of an investment in a business or company. Most socially responsible investors check companies out using ESG criteria to screen investments. The relationship between ESG and the board of directors of companies is still being defined. Discussions around the "G" (i.e., governance) are often spearheaded by the nominating and governance committee with involvement from the full board— particularly when assessing how these risks integrate with the enterprise risk management (ERM) program or impact long-term strategy. ESG became mainstream in 2020. Using ESG metrics is an extended version of Marxist Critical Race Theory—scoring, reshaping, and mastering the financial world using Marxist tactics. ESG systems, sustainable investment, and forcing the world to adopt "green" energy sources are all essential elements of the Great Reset plan to transform the world.

The Great Reset

COVID-19 could destroy the economy and lead to the birth of a new system. The World Economic Forum (https://www.weforum.org) and the book *COVID-19: THE GREAT RESET* by Klaus Schwab and Thierry Malleret assure us that the modern world after the pandemic will be better, more inclusive, more equitable, and more respectful of Mother Nature once we reset the present social/economic system and replace it with a new and better one.

Chapter 2 of the book shows how past epidemics have altered society and how COVID-19 can do the same today, and that germ phobia will reshape society. Chapter 4 calls for a restructuring of the world's economy and a global government. A sub category of the World Economic Forum is the Centre for the Fourth Industrial Revolution where societies and personal lives are highlighted. In their conclusion, on page 243, they ask the question: Could COVID-19 have the force to ignite profound changes?"

According to the World Economic Forum, COVID-19 will usher in the Great Reset, which will be imposed by violent shocks like conflicts and even revolutions. The Forum is an avenue for the world elite to put us in bondage and debt by eliminating private property, the free enterprise system, installing fake democracy by stamping out real democracy, controlling the media with their propaganda, and replacing Judeo-Christian western values with paganism.

We can't grow the economy without growing the debt, and debt is the very thing that will bring down the economy. An increase in debt Economist Norm Franz once stated, "*Gold is the money of kings, silver is the money of gentlemen, barter is the money of peasants—but debt is the money of slaves.*"

The Great Reset is a coordinated plan that has been years in the making before the virus; it is a fresh coat of lipstick on an old pig; it is a social and economic world transformation. The Great Reset will centralize power in fewer hands through Orwellian surveillance technologies. Yuval Noah Harari wrote an article for the *Financial Times* titled *The World After the Coronavirus*. The opening sentence reads This storm will pass. But the choices we make now could change our lives for years to come...they will shape not just our health care systems but also our economy, politics, and culture" Technology has made it possible for the government to monitor us and punish anyone who dare break the rules.

Hegelian Dialectic

"Hegel's dialectics" refers to the dialectical method of argument employed by the 19th Century German philosopher Georg Wilhelm Friedrich Hegel, which relies on a contradictory process between opposing sides. The Hegelian dialectic is a framework for guiding our thoughts and actions that lead us to a pre-determined solution to a problem. If we do not understand how the Hegelian dialectic shapes our perceptions of the world, then we can become victims of the perpetrators who wish to control our thoughts and actions—unwittingly, we help to implement the pre-determined outcome which ultimately leads to our bondage.

Black Swan Events

The term Black Swan originates from the belief that there are only white swans. However, the opinion changed after a Dutch explorer discovered black swans in Australia—people consider low probability but high impact occurrences as black swan events. Nine-eleven, the threat of global warming, and COVID-19 policies are black swan events.

Red Herring Events

A red herring event is an event that leads people to wrong conclusions by constructing a false narrative.

Critical Race Theory

Critical race theory (CRT) is a movement based on the premise that race is not natural but a socially constructed (culturally invented) category that perpetrators use to oppress and exploit people of color. Critical Race Theory is a Marxist framework that views society only through the lens of race-based oppression.

Critical race theory is opposed to traditional values. There was a time when a country identified itself by ancestry and common ethnic nationality. Not so for America. If America abandons its political and economic structures, it will lose its identity more thoroughly than a country defined by a common ethnic and cultural background. The fabric of America's identity are the institutions of personal liberty, free contracts, jury trials, uncensored news media, regular and free elections, open competition, private property rights, religious freedom, and habeas corpus.

Woke Movement and Cancel Culture

Woke is a term that originated in the United States, referring to a perceived awareness of issues that concern social justice and racial justice. It is like saying we have to wake people up from their preconceived notions of race, particularly white privilege, but it can also include anything contrary to the official narrative. Cancel culture is a modern form of ostracism in which someone is thrust out of social or professional circles, whether it be online, on social media, or in person. Those who are subject to this ostracism are said to have been "cancelled."

According to a new mathematics teaching resource guide, Math is embedded with white supremacy culture that must be rooted out by the social justice police and consequently transformed to fit their teaching protocols. Oregon's Department of Education approved the controversial teacher's resource titled, A Pathway to Equitable Math Instruction. The 82-page manual is not a math curriculum but rather a toolkit for teachers designed to influence the climate of education by helping teachers identify ways where white supremacy culture shows up in teaching mathematics to students in grades 6-8.

Following are examples of the Woke Movement and the Cancel Culture. Angela Davis is a left-wing activist who has been deeply involved in Communist politics, feminism movements, and other radical causes. Although Butler University scheduled her to be the lead speaker at a Joint Struggle and Collective Liberation event, the university canceled her appearance because she supported Palestinians. When Georgia passed a bill requiring voters to provide photo identification when they vote, Major League Baseball announced moving the All-Star Game from Atlanta to Denver, Colorado. United Airlines has abandoned merit-based hiring practices to appeal to the Woke Movement by notifying that fifty percent of pilot trainees will be women and minorities. The US government has threatened to boycott the 2022 Beijing Olympics over China's Uighur Muslims' treatment. The Cancel culture has convinced the Cleveland Indians baseball team to change their name after 100 years.

CHAPTER 1
OVERVIEW

AUSTRIANS vs KEYNESIANS

Austrian economists believe that the price mechanism can best allocate resources and that too much government intervention is harmful to the economy. The Austrian School derives its name from its founders, who were citizens of the Austrian Empire in the mid-1800s, including Carl Manger, Ludwig von Mises, and Frederick Hayek.

Keynesians get their name from John Maynard Keynes (1883-1946), who had a book published in 1936 called *The General Theory of Employment, Interest, and Money*. Keynes made the argument that if we can manage demand, we can manage the economy. He argued that there are times when the economy tends toward less than full-employment equilibrium and that investments may not be sufficient to maintain growth. At these times, the government and the Federal Reserve (our central bank) should stimulate the economy.

Austrians and Keynesians have opinions and make value judgments. When economists express opinions, they indicate how they believe things should be, not necessarily stating the facts. These normative statements involve value judgments about what should be or what ought to happen. Should the government raise the minimum wage? Should the government increase welfare spending? Should the government extend unemployment benefits? Should the government expand social welfare programs, or should we leave benevolent programs to the private sector? Economists try to explain how the world works and hopefully, as policy advisors, improve the world. Most economists view themselves as scientists seeking the truth about how the world works.

Keep in mind that it is not likely that even the most objective economists can be unbiased in their assessment of economic events, even though they may try to be fair and impartial. Because economists have strong beliefs, they tend to emphasize data or evidence that tends to support ideas consistent with their belief system, putting less weight on evidence that may be contrary to their point of view. This tendency to be biased is human nature. Despite this bias, economists try to understand how things work and then describe what would happen if certain things changed. Although economists do frequently have opposite views on economic policy, they do agree on the principles.

PITFALLS TO AVOID

Consider these two pitfalls of economic analysis. The first is not to confuse correlation with causation. If two events usually occur together, this does not mean that the one caused the other.

For example, when you were young, a rooster's crowing woke you up every morning, followed shortly by the sunrise. You came to associate the crowing with the rising sun and believed the first action caused the second. The same is true in our analysis of economic events: the relationship between two variables may not be as apparent as we first assume.

The second pitfall is the fallacy of composition. This fallacy states that even if something is valid for an individual, it is not necessarily true for groups. For example, suppose you are in a football stadium when your team's quarterback throws a long pass. To get a better view of the receiver, you stand up. But what happens if everyone around you stands up? The same is true when you arrive early at Best Buy to purchase the new iPhone.

FACTORS OF PRODUCTION

The four factors of production are land, labor, capital, and entrepreneurship. Land is anything from the earth that helps solve the economic problem, such as freshwater, soil, timber, minerals, oil, and metals. Labor occurs when people work to provide a good or service for market transactions. Cutting your neighbor's grass for money is an example of labor. Cutting your grass is not labor. Capital consists of buildings, equipment, and machines used to produce other goods. For instance, economists consider a carpenter's hammer capital because the carpenter uses it as a tool to build something that ends in a market transaction. Human capital is the knowledge and skills needed to work with capital.

Entrepreneurship

Entrepreneurs see opportunities where other people may not, they are willing to take risks to start and grow a business, and they have a vision and strive to overcome obstacles to fulfill their dream. They have learned the lesson of delayed gratification, and they are not afraid of hard work and sacrifice, and they know that the way to succeed is to help other people. You demonstrate the characteristics of entrepreneurship because you are a person with dreams and goals.

Business owners can earn more money, have more free time, and enjoy more security than wage earners because entrepreneurs can duplicate themselves through other people. For example, suppose an entrepreneur employs 100 people who work eight hours in a single day. Employees receive credit for what they produce in the first seven hours; that is, whatever revenue their labor brings into the business in the first seven hours goes to them in the form of wages, insurance, retirement benefits, etc. The entrepreneur gets credit for what the worker produces in the eighth hour. This duplication is equivalent to the entrepreneur working 100 hours in a single day. He can be on vacation and still get credit for working 100 hours each day, and his security is not dependent on his ability to perform.

Duplication comes in different forms, such as owning rental property or earning interest on money in savings. Entrepreneurs can replicate themselves through renters because a fraction of what renters earn goes to the landlord. People can duplicate themselves through earning interest because borrowers work to pay the saver interest.

Entrepreneurs follow the Law of Use, which recognizes that if a person has money, he receives more money, and the more money he has, the more he will receive. If he does not have money, the system will take money away from him. For example, when you put money into a savings account, you can earn interest. On the other hand, if you cannot pay cash for a car, you have to borrow money and pay interest; that is, interest takes your money away.

Entrepreneurs also follow the Law of Reciprocity, which recognizes that whatever you give away, you keep, and whatever you keep, you lose. Does this also sound like a riddle? Let me explain. What two things do you want in life? Why are you in college? You are a college student because you want more money and time. So what two things are you giving up by attending college? Yes, you guessed it—money and time!

More than anything else, entrepreneurship is an attitude, a perspective, a way of thinking. Entrepreneurs know that the key to all wealth building is the principle of paying yourself first. George S. Clason, who wrote *The Richest Man in Babylon*, published in 1926, explains the principle of paying yourself first. The book tells a story of how a poor scribe in Babylon learns the concept of wealth building. We will pick up the story on page 12, where a wealthy man, Algamish, comes to Arkad, the scribe. Algamish needs some clay tablets carved by the next day. Because this is a huge task, Arkad makes a deal with Algamish.

I found the road to wealth when I decided that a part of all I earned was mine to keep. If you did keep but one-tenth of all you

earn, how much would you have in ten years? Wealth is like a tree,
it grows from a tiny seed.

Entrepreneurs also know the importance of self-sacrifice.
David Siegel, the owner of Westgate Resorts, is an example of this
principle. Following is a partial copy of an email he sent to his
employees and posted on the internet. Below are excerpts from that
email:

> *I started this company over 42 years*
> *ago. At that time, I lived in a very modest*
> *home. We didn't eat in fancy restaurants or*
> *take expensive vacations because every dollar*
> *I made went back into this company. I was*
> *married to my business - hard work, discipline,*
> *and sacrifice.*

Who Are The Entrepreneurs?

Most entrepreneurs live in the same town all of their adult
life. They own a small factory, a chain of stores, or a service
company. They marry once and remain married. They live next
door to people with a fraction of their wealth and are compulsive
savers and investors. Eighty percent of America's millionaires did
not inherit their wealth.

INFLATION AND UNEMPLOYMENT

Inflation, defined as a general rise in the average price
level, diminishes buying power as real incomes decline, demand
declines, and most everyone's standard of living shrinks. As

consumer demand declines, inventories build, leading to less production and fewer employees. Inflation is most harmful when it is high and volatile because of its impact on consumer demand and business investments.

All businesses need an inventory, but companies cut back production and lay off resources when their stock becomes excessive. Economists like to quip that a recession is when your neighbor is unemployed, and a depression is when you are unemployed! The government declares a recession when the economy experiences at least two consecutive quarters (three-month periods) of a decline in the real gross domestic product (real GDP). Economists define GDP as the market value of new, domestically produced, final goods and services. Four sectors make up GDP: the consumption sector (C), the investment sector (I), the government sector (G), and the foreign sector, which is the difference between imports and exports (X-M). The four critical elements of GDP are:

- Market value – economists calculate GDP by multiplying the prices of goods and services by their quantities. Economists adjust real GDP for inflation in order to get an accurate comparison from one time period to the next.
- New – economists only include goods that producers make in the current accounting period, which is normally the current calendar year.

- Domestically produced.
- Final goods and services – economists only include the final value in the measure of GDP. This eliminates the problem of double counting.

Rather than relying on government statistics, most economists use the National Bureau of Economic Research (NBER) definition of a recession. Ever since 1920, the NBER has reported on general economic conditions in the United States. Over time, the NBER developed a reputation for measuring the economy's performance in an evenhanded and practical way. There are two reasons why economists generally prefer the NBER measure. First, the government only measures GDP quarterly, and the NBER calculates GDP monthly. Second, the official GDP numbers are subject to frequent revisions, making it difficult to assess trends.

The NBER defines a recession as "a significant decline in activity spread across the economy, lasting more than a few months." The NBER focuses on the following:

- Industrial production.
- Employment.
- Real income (income adjusted for inflation).
- Sales at both wholesale and retail levels.

CONFLICTING GOALS

The pursuit of income equality and fairness may be noble,

but when these goals take precedence over growth, unemployment ensues, and economies stagnate. Once the economy spirals downward, economic problems escalate, unemployment worsens, choices diminish, opportunity diminishes, and pain results. Ultimately, we must relearn the lessons of growth by saving and investing and relinquishing other priorities. Once the economy grows, we can afford other goals such as income equality, a cleaner environment, and enhanced opportunity.

Growth

Why is growth necessary? Growth is essential because time is a cruel taskmaster. If we do not grow, things deteriorate, and the allocation problem intensifies as society jostles for scarce goods and services. People with money, job security, and political contacts prosper at the expense of everyone else. When this happens, young people, such as recent high school and college graduates, bear the greatest burden.

Modern Europe is experiencing slow growth because of other priorities. For example, in Italy, it is unlawful for a company with more than 15 employees to fire anyone. France is another country with anti-growth laws. The high minimum wage and heavy taxes on wealthy individuals and large corporations have caused high unemployment levels. The Spanish government has instituted policies that guarantee 22 days of paid vacation annually, 15 days to get married, and two to four days when anyone in an employee's family has a wedding, birth, hospitalization, or death. Sick employees can receive most or all of their wages for 18 consecutive months if they have a doctor's note.

Can a country support liberal social policies without experiencing unemployment? Yes, anything is possible if a county's growth is strong enough. Most everyone can share prosperity with an ever-expanding pie, but a shrinking pie will lead to stagnation.

Minimizing Negative Externalities

Negative externalities are the unwanted by-products of industry, such as pollution, unsafe working conditions, an uneven distribution of wealth, and income inequality. So, what resources should we apply to growth and which to reducing negative externalities?

Affordable Housing

The lofty goal of affordable housing for low-income people precipitated the financial collapse of 2007-2008 when Congress encouraged homeownership for almost everyone. When the housing market turned down, homeowners walked away from their obligations, with devastating consequences for the rest of the economy.

SELF-INTEREST

Adam Smith, known as the father of economics, authored *An Inquiry into the Nature and Causes of the Wealth of Nations*, published in 1776. He explained how the invisible hand of self-interest in free markets directs the flow of resources. He explained how the profit motive, or the producer's self-interest, works to satisfy consumers' wants.

> *It is not due to the benevolence of the butcher, the brewer, or the baker, that we expect our dinner, but from regard to their own self-interest. We address ourselves, not to their humanity but to their self-love, and never talk to them of our own necessities but of their own advantages.*

DEMOCRACY vs REPUBLIC

What is the difference between a democracy and a republic? In a pure democracy, the majority of voters rule over the minority. But a republic is a government based on law. Our form of government is a republic tempered by democracy.

A significant blow to the republic was Senate Majority Leader Harry Reid's decision in 2012 to undo 200 years of precedent that required a supermajority to change Senate rules, which previously required 60 votes out of one hundred and fifty votes. To speed the approval of executive appointments and judicial nominations, Senator Reid forced a vote of 52 to 48 that allows the Senate majority to change the rules whenever it wants. If a majority can change the rules or laws whenever they want, and the minority has no recourse, the republic is on the road to ruin.

The following story, which takes place during the 1400s, illustrates the loss of personal freedom. Maria is a sixteen-year-old daughter of a wealthy merchant in Madrid, Spain, and a devout

Catholic. She and her two brothers go to dinner at a local inn. Her brothers order pork, but she orders chicken. An official of Queen Isabella, a member of the group "who asks questions," witnesses this from across the room. His job is to seek out heretics. Why does she not order pork? She must be a Jew or at least accept Jewish beliefs. The authorities arrest, torture, and throw her into prison. Her family comes and pays a large sum of money, hoping to rescue their daughter. Queen Isabella keeps the money but does not release the daughter. She does go free ten years later without her youth and beauty. Maria finds her home, but the government has killed her family and confiscated their possessions. She dies within a year after begging in the streets. The following is an excerpt from *The Story of Liberty*, page 94, by Charles Coffin, published in 1879.

> *Through the waning summer months of 1492 the stricken Jews take their departure: five hundred thousand are driven from the country! With them go the thrift and industry of Spain. Isabella, Ferdinand, and the Pope, through the Holy Office, have possession of the property, but estates without tenants bring no income to the treasury. In driving them out, Ferdinand and Isabella kill the goose that lays the golden egg.*

The above story illustrates what can occur when a ruling class imposes its will on society and personifies the age-old struggle between freedom and tyranny. It was against such an oppressive system that America rebelled against England during the 1600s and most of the 1700s. During this time, Thomas Jefferson said, *When governments fear the people, there is liberty, but when the people fear the government, there is tyranny.*

The American Revolution

The strife between England and the American colonies began in the decade between 1763 and 1773. During these years, Britain enacted the Grenville and Townsend Acts, which favored British businesses over American businesses. The colonists reacted with boycotts, fiery speeches, violence, and protest meetings. Britain did repeal some regulations but persisted in strengthening its control over the colonies. There was a growing concern that England was violating "man's natural rights."

Below are some excerpts from the Virginia Bill of Rights of the year 1776.

1. *That all men are by nature equally free and independent, and have certain inherent rights, of which, when they enter into a state of society, they cannot by any compact deprive or divest their posterity; namely, the enjoyment of life and liberty, with means of acquiring and possessing property, and pursuing and obtaining happiness and safety.*

2. *That all power is vested in, and consequently derived, from the people; that magistrates are their trustees and servants, and at all times amenable to them.*

Our forefathers recognized that our rights come from God and that liberty is fragile. Following is a quote from the Declaration of Independence of 1776:

We hold these truths to be self-evident, that all men are created equal, that they are endowed by their Creator with certain unalienable Rights that among these are Life, Liberty, and the pursuit of Happiness. That to secure these rights, Governments are instituted among Men, deriving their just powers from the consent of the governed, that whenever any form of Government becomes destructive to these ends, it is the Right of the people to alter or to abolish it, and to institute new Government, laying its foundation on such principles and organizing its powers in such form as to them shall seem most likely to affect their Safety and Happiness.

COMPETITION AND PRICES

Once a company invents something that sells, others will

say, *maybe we can compete and make money too.* So how do you thrive in a free market economy? You learn to reduce your costs, and then you lower your prices to increase sales.

COMPETITION AND PROFITS

Economists define price as the rate at which buyers and sellers exchange money for goods and services, and they determine the cost as the money businesses pay for their inputs. Economists define revenue as the money gained by selling goods and services, and profit is the difference between revenues and costs. When a company lowers costs and prices more than its competitors, it gains market share and profit.

THE PRICE MECHANISM

In a free market, the price mechanism determines the free flow of goods and services. However, the federal government's expanding role has eroded this free flow of goods and services, as demonstrated in the loanable funds market. In a free market, the demand and supply of money would determine interest rates and undermine the free market system. But in today's world, central banks determine interest rates and therefore undermine the free market. What are the consequences of the United States moving away from a free-market economy? You cannot answer this question unless you understand how the price mechanism works in free markets. In a free market system, prices serve three purposes: they convey information, they give incentives, and they determine income distribution.

Prices Convey Information

Producers must decide what consumers are able and willing to buy. If a product becomes popular, demand will overcome supply, and the market price will increase as consumers bid against one another. When prices rise, producers know consumers want more of the product, and the higher prices will provide incentives to increase the quantity supplied. On the other hand, if the goods are not popular, there will be a surplus on the market, and as retail prices fall, producers will reduce the quantity supplied.

The Price Mechanism and Incentives

Consumers may want more of a product, and producers will be motivated to produce more—but where will they get the money for raw materials, machines, buildings, and employees? The money will come from higher prices and higher profits. If prices did not increase, the producer might not be able to satisfy consumers' wants. Therefore, the price mechanism gives incentives to the producer to satisfy consumer wants and needs. The price mechanism rewards successful entrepreneurs with profits and punishes others with losses. This system of rewards and punishments is what makes the economy grow and prosper.

FREE MARKETS vs PLANNING

What happens when the price mechanism breaks down, blurring price signals and skewing incentives? The free market falters, growth stagnates, and centralized planning proliferates.

CHAPTER 1: OVERVIEW

Planning limits choices as the government decides who gets what and how much. America's forefathers, the men who birthed this nation, realized that a planned economy is the biggest threat to individual freedom. The Constitution limits government power and minimizes centralized planning by dividing power among the three branches of government. Societies need order, and that order can come from the rule of law or by the iron fist of centralized planning. On January 4, 2011, the House of Representatives passed a rule requiring that members must cite the constitutional authority for every piece of legislation they write.

The fourth unofficial branch of government is a knowledgeable, and trustworthy media. Unfortunately the mainline news and popular social media platforms no longer represent honest and true news. When investigative reporting wanes and the system restricts the free press, we stand to lose our personal freedom. In the eighteenth century, Alexander Tyler described the following stages of democracy:

1) From bondage to spiritual freedom,

2) From spiritual faith to great courage

3) From courage to liberty

4) From liberty to abundance

5) From abundance to complacency

6) From complacency to apathy

7) From Apathy to dependence

8) From dependence to bondage

UNEMPLOYMENT

Warehouses pile up with unsold inventory when production outstrips demand, and unemployment feeds upon itself as businesses cut production. Eventually, a company may reduce its prices, but its priority is to match production with demand. History is a series of economic booms and busts as the economy adjusts to an ever-changing landscape. The question is, "what role should government play when unemployment threatens prosperity?" Whereas Keynesian economists tend to favor government intervention, Austrian economists have a laissez-faire attitude toward economics. Laissez-faire is a French term that means "leave alone."

World War I lasted from 1914 to 1918, during which time the demand for commodities increased. However, in the years following the war, America experienced the Depression of 1921 as the world's demand for American commodities declined. By the time the government intervened, the economy had recovered, and the decade of the roaring twenties had gotten underway. The 1920s was a decade of many inventions, innovations, and rapid growth. One fundamental philosophical belief that eventually led to the Depression of the 1930s was the belief that by keeping wages low and prices high, profits increased. Low wages and high prices led to increased profits, at least for a while, but the same also led to unemployment as demand lagged behind production. Compounding the problem was the high profits encouraged risky investments leading the way to the Great Depression. The build-up of excessive inventories caused a recession but was not a reason for the Great Depression of the 1930s. What happened next is an example of government policies that, even though well-intentioned, made matters worse.

The Smoot-Hawley Tariff of the early 1930s, the highest protective tariff in U.S. history, had the opposite effect on the economy than politicians expected. Instead of Americans buying more American made products, they bought fewer products.

The Federal Reserve's attempt to decrease the money supply to increase interest rates was the second cause of the Great Depression. The Fed was hoping to attract foreign money with the higher interest rates in the 1930s. However, the high interest rates caused a decline in consumer demand, worsening unemployment.

An increase in government spending and a reduction in revenue led to the rise in the national debt. Fearful that an increase in the national debt would harm the economy, President Herbert Hoover raised taxes to balance the budget, resulting in a decrease in consumer demand and an increase in unemployment.

By 1933, total output in the United States fell one-third from its previous level, and unemployment reached 25 percent. Living conditions worsened because there were no government unemployment benefits and many workers experienced lower wages. As the depression spread to other countries, suffering intensified, leading the way to massive changes.

In 1934, Franklin D. Roosevelt took over the presidency and immediately enacted his New Deal Program, expanding the federal government's role. Roosevelt ordered the Treasury to sell bonds to fund his programs. These policies were consistent with Keynesian economics.

DIFFERENCES OF OPINION

The government played a minor role in the brief depression of 1920-1921 and a major role in the much longer depression of the 1930s. So was the Great Depression of the 1930s caused by a failure of free enterprise or government failure? Several years ago, a prominent economist, the late Milton Friedman, asserted that government policy caused the depression. According to Professor Friedman, the government turned a recession into a depression because of mismanaged monetary and fiscal policies. Professor Friedman believed that the New Deal ushered in a series of big government programs that inhibited economic growth. Keynesian economists, however, believe that it was Roosevelt's New Deal Programs that prevented a communist revolution and saved capitalism.

Here is a quote from John Maynard Keynes:

The ideas of economists and political philosophers, both when they are right and when they are wrong, are more powerful than is commonly understood. Indeed, the world is ruled by little else. Practical men, who believe themselves to be quite exempt from any intellectual influences, are usually the slaves of some defunct economist.

Since the Depression of the 1930s, we have experienced an ever-larger federal government and the national debt has skyrocketed. Keynesian economics has held sway during this time, and Austrian economists' beliefs have not gained widespread support. Conservatives tend to be more suspicious of big government than are liberals.

SUMMARY

The key to a free market is self-interest. Profit motivates producers to give consumers what they want, and competition ensures reasonable prices. An entrepreneur is a person who has a dream, who organizes and manages any enterprise, has learned the lesson of delayed gratification, and is willing to risk.

In a free and unregulated market, prices transmit information from the consumer to the producer, give incentives to the producer to satisfy consumer demand, and provide the financial capital to satisfy society's wants and needs. When the price mechanism dictates a higher price, producers will increase that good or service. The quantity supplied increases because producers can make more money at higher prices.

CHAPTER 2
DECISIONS

S hould you buy a new car? Should you put your savings in a bank, the stock market, or gold? Should you sell your shares of stock now or later? Should you paint your room or hire someone? How many soda pops will you buy to maximize your level of satisfaction? As a producer, how many widgets should you produce to maximize your profit? Is it a good idea for the federal government to mandate ethanol in gasoline? Should the market determine interest rates, or should the Federal Reserve? Should we continue to use coal or seek alternative energy sources? How should society assess the distribution of income? What authority should the federal government have over states' rights? Ah, so many decisions it makes the head spin!

Absolute and Comparative Advantage

Should you paint your bedroom yourself or hire someone? Let's analyze this question using the concepts of absolute and comparative. Absolute advantage occurs when you can do something using fewer resources than anyone else; comparative advantage is when you can do something with lower opportunity costs than someone else. Economists make decisions based on comparative advantage, not absolute advantage.

Should you paint your bedroom yourself or hire someone? If you could make $50 an hour in the best alternative endeavor, you would be giving up $50 each hour it took to paint the room yourself, which would be your opportunity cost. If you hire someone at $20 an hour and you work during that hour, you gain $30. However, if you can only earn $15 an hour in the best alternative endeavor, you will lose $5 an hour if you hire someone to paint the room.

Suppose you are an independent automobile mechanic who charges $25.00 per hour and you work eight hours a day - five days a week. After several days, you find that your garage needs cleaning and organizing. Each hour you spend cleaning the shop, you incur an opportunity cost of $25.00. One day, Ed, a high school student, comes by asking for work. You realize you could hire Ed to clean the shop for $10.00 an hour. Even though you have an absolute advantage in cleaning the garage, you do not have a comparative advantage because of your high opportunity cost of $25.00 an hour. Ed has a low opportunity cost because this is the only job he can find. If you hire Ed and spend the hour repairing cars, you are better off by $15 an hour.

DECISIONS

The four decision-making groups are consumers, business, foreigners, and government. The interaction among these groups determines how society allocates resources and who gets what and how much. In a free-market, individuals make decisions; the interaction between consumer demand and supply is paramount.

Even in a free market economy, there is a need for a strong central government that would provide us with a strong national defense, promote merit goods, help poor and disadvantaged people, and protect society from negative externalities, such as pollution. With a dictatorial form of government or an oligarchy, where a group rules society, economic decisions would be more centralized. Now let's look more closely at the four groups that make up our economy.

Consumption Sector

The consumption sector is the largest and most stable GDP sector because consumers tend to make decisions based on their perceived long-term income. Consider a family whose $100,000 a year income falls to $70,000. Will the family's spending habits adapt to the lower income? Eventually, yes, but human nature being what it is, makes people gravitate toward the familiar. In other words, the family will continue to eat out at restaurants, attend the aquatic center, and watch cable TV. The family continues their previous lifestyle by taking money out of savings, something economists call dissaving. Eventually, they will take money out of their real savings, such as selling stock shares and the boat they rarely use. After this, they will borrow other people's savings by going into debt spending downward to match their new lower income.

Investment Sector

Businesses can be sole proprietorships, partnerships, or corporations. The most popular business type is a sole proprietorship, a company with a single owner who has the right to all proceeds and bears unlimited liability for its debts. Whereas the consumption sector is very slow to change, the investment sector is unstable because entrepreneurs make decisions based on their expected return rate. Investors need the assurance that an investment will be profitable before risking their financial capital; negative expectations, increased in costs, taxes, and regulations will discourage investments.

Foreign Sector

The foreign sector establishes trade among nations. If Americans were better than anyone else at making handmade wicker baskets, should they spend time, money, and energy making them? The answer is no because each hour spent making a basket is an hour taken from elsewhere, such as technology. America's advanced technology, educated workforce, and modern infrastructure, make spending time in technology more profitable than making baskets.

Suppose you own a widget business and you have a choice of staying in the U.S. or moving to Mexico. The hourly wages in America and Mexico are $20.00 and $2.00 an hour, respectfully. Should you relocate to Mexico, where the hourly wage is less? The answer is "that all depends" because you have to consider both inputs and outputs. The hourly wage would be the input, and the number of widgets produced per hour would be the output. If the American worker makes 20 widgets per hour and the Mexican worker one widget per hour, the American worker is less expensive on a per-unit basis.

In a capital-intensive industry, the advantages of superior infrastructure, advanced telecommunications network, a highly educated and skilled workforce, and modern technology would offset low wages' benefits.

High tech companies stay in America, and low tech companies, like textile companies, relocate to places like Bangladesh where wages are meager. Seamstresses in Bangladesh fashion garments for global brands for a monthly salary of only $38.

Government Sector

Federal, state, and local governments make up the government sector. The United States Constitution allocated to each government a level of sovereignty. When Benjamin Franklin exited the Constitutional Convention, a woman asked him, *What have you given us?* His response was, "*Republic, Ma'am if you can keep it.* Notice that he did not say, *We have given you a democracy*.

The Constitution establishes a form of government that is a democracy in a republic whereby the majority rule, but law tempers their authority. When we pledge allegiance to the flag, we do not say ... *to the democracy for which it stands*. We say ... *to the republic for which it stands*. James Madison warned us against the dangers of democracy when he said:

> *Democracies have ever been spectacles of turbulence and contention; democracies have ever been found incompatible with personal security and rights of property,*

*and have in general been as short in their
lives as they have been violent in their
deaths.*

Alexander Hamilton was a Founding Father, soldier, economist, political philosopher, one of America's first constitutional lawyers, and the first United States Secretary of the Treasury. Samuel Adams was an American diplomat, political philosopher, one of the Founding Fathers of the United States, and a signer of the Declaration of Independence.

Alexander Hamilton: *We are a republican form of government. We will never achieve real liberty in despotism or extremes of democracy.*

Samuel Adams: *Democracy never lasts long. It soon wastes, exhausts and murders itself.*

WHAT KIND OF ECONOMIC SYSTEM?

The different forms of government are monarchy (dictatorship), oligarchy, democracy, and republic. One person rules monarchies and dictatorships, but these government forms are rare since monarchs have councils and dictatorships usually have bureaucrats. The most common form of governments are oligarchies where a powerful few people possess all the power.

All societies have to answer the three basic questions of what, how, and for whom to produce. There is a blend between the government making these decisions in almost all situations and the free market deciding how to allocate society's scarce resources. Because history does not stand still and because life is a flow situation where events are in flux, sometimes market forces prevail, and at other times government edict holds sway. For example, the government might pass laws contrary to free market dictates and mandate greater solar power use instead of coal.

John Stuart Mill, a philosopher and economist who lived in the 1800s, recognized that the market system was about production, but not necessarily about distribution. In his famous book, *Principles of Political Economy*, published in 1848, Mill states:

> *The things once there, mankind individually or collectively, can do with them as they please. They can place them at the disposal of whomever they please, and on whatever terms. . . . Even what a person has produced by his individual toil, unaided by anyone, he cannot keep, unless by the permission of society. . . . The distribution of wealth, therefore, depends on the laws and customs of society.*

Yes, we can redistribute goods and services, but at what point will this tinkering lead to inefficiencies? At what point does redistribution impede growth and impair productivity? If the government interferes with the price mechanism too much, price signals blur, and the economy shrinks. This practice of government supplanting the free market encourages crony capitalism. Crony capitalism describes an economy in which business success depends on close relationships between business people and government officials. Along with crony capitalism, we experience more "rent-seeking" and "moral hazard."

Rent-seeking activities do not benefit society; they redistribute resources from the taxpayers to the special-interest group. Moral hazard occurs when the system protects someone, and therefore, that person will act differently than if he did not have protection. The idea of a corporation being too big or too important to fail represents a moral hazard. If the public and the management believe a company will be the recipient of a financial bailout, management may engage in risky behavior to pursue profits.

Government safety nets tend to create moral hazards that lead to more risk-taking. Who pays for a dollar that the government spends? If the dollar comes from taxes, then-current tax laws govern who pays. If the government borrows the money, borrowers pay in the form of higher interest rates. If the government, in conjunction with the Federal Reserve, creates the money, people on fixed incomes pay the most because of inflation.

High taxes, especially taxes on capital, and excessive government regulations can also cripple a free market system. With growing unemployment, demands for action become louder as everyone blames others for the problems. The situation worsens as events affect groups differently, and each group wants to game the system.

ECONOMIC GOALS

Economists have identified eight basic goals:

- Economic growth
- Full employment
- Stable prices
- Efficiency
- Fair sharing of goods and services
- Minimizing negative externalities
- Economic freedom
- Economic security

Growth

Most Americans enjoy a high standard of living, but the economy must grow to maintain this standard. Society neglects pro-growth policies to its peril. The consequence of not replacing the goods we currently have is to experience less and less with each passing day as things deteriorate. That well-running car you are driving will eventually deteriorate, as will everything else. Failure to grow will lead to an ever more unequal distribution of wealth, a decline in society's standard of living, and civil unrest.

A country's per capita living standard depends on its population growth. If we stand still but the birth rate declines, society is better off on a per capita basis. Likewise, if we replace what we currently have, but the population increases, we are worse off on a per capita basis. Even though the world is experiencing lower birth rates, life expectancies are longer than in earlier years.

CHAPTER 2: DECISIONS

The government can help pro-growth policies with business-friendly regulations or a tax system that encourages people to save, take risks, and invest. Germany offers a compelling example of pro-growth policies under Gerhard Schröder in recent times and Ludwig Erhard in the 1940s. By 1948, the German people had lived under price controls for twelve years and rationing for nine years. Adolf Hitler had imposed price controls on the German people in 1936 so that his administration could get war materials at artificially low prices. Later, in 1939, the government imposed rationing on the nation. In 1945, the Allied Control Authority, formed by the United States, Britain, France, and the Soviet Union, agreed to support Hitler's price controls. The low food prices discouraged farmers from bringing their products to market, leading to food shortages and famine.

Meanwhile, Ludwig Erhard and the Social Free Market School believed in free markets, along with a slightly progressive income tax and limited monopoly. Sometimes natural monopolies trump competition, such as power and cable companies where the government restricts competition in return for price controls.

Opposed to the Social Free Market School was the Social Democratic Party (SDP), who wanted a strong central government. The SDP argued that decontrol of prices and currency reform would be unproductive. Agreeing with the SDP were labor unions, the British authorities, most West German manufacturing interests, and American authorities. However, Ludwig Erhard won this debate in the 1940s and abolished most price controls. Along with currency reform and decontrol of prices, the government also cut taxes, paving the way to a booming economy. The government reestablished money as the preferred medium of exchange in free markets. Output continued to grow after 1948, and by 1958, industrial production was more than four times its previous annual rate. Economists in the 1950s regarded this economic growth as a miracle.

Ludwig Erhard understood the harmful effects that inflation had on the economy. He illustrated that price controls and high tax rates lead to poverty and misery and that free-market policies enhance productivity gains and prosperity. Similarly, Gerhard Schröder, who was German chancellor from 1998 to 2005, lowered taxes, revamped unemployment benefits, and streamlined labor laws. Economists have credited Mr. Schröder's shakedown of the welfare state with insulating Germany against the debt problems that would later occur in Southern Europe. In most of Europe, there has been little evidence that these reforms have rubbed off.

Growth is the only way out of Europe's debt predicament. But what are the best growth policies? The Keynesian consensus, which has dominated world economic councils, believes "growth" is mostly a function of government spending even if a country raises taxes to pay for it and that spending cuts are equivalent to lower growth. This emphasis on government spending is a top-down approach to problems, whereas Austrian economists tend to favor policies that grow the economy from the bottom up. Keynesians tend to support macroeconomic policies, and Austrians tend to favor microeconomic policies to promote growth.

Austrian economists believe that America's economic problems stem from government failure rather than a failure of the free market. According to Austrian thought, a primary tenant of growth is a predictable future, yet government policies often sew confusion and uncertainty into the mix.

The Alternative Minimum Tax (AMT), which Congress passed in 1969, is a parallel tax system alongside our present system, under which high-income taxpayers do not benefit from deductions and exemptions. In response to the people's hardship and inflation Congress changes the rules. This practice of changing the rules each year causes confusion and uncertainty regarding high-income people's tax decisions. Austrian economists tend to be suspicious when the government changes definitions at critical times. To make inflation look better, the Bureau of Labor Statistics revised the consumer price index (CPI) description by taking out price increases of food and energy. Because the benefits received by government social programs are adjusted each year by the CPI, these payments to recipients are less than they would be under the old definition of CPI. In 2014 the Census Bureau changed how it counts health insurance while ObamaCare was roiling the insurance markets.

The Keynesian mantra of "timely, targeted, and temporary" tax cuts and spending is the second and biggest mistake. Austrians believe that Congress cannot calculate the right amount and timing of temporary tax cuts and spending. Keynesians believe that tax cuts must be brief to not add to the "long-term" deficit.

Keynesian policies are the norm today, but this philosophy has not always been popular. President Ronald Reagan supported Austrian economics in the 1980s and was a student of F.A. Hayek (1899-1992). He often quoted Hayek's famous book *The Road to*

Serfdom, published in 1944, warning of a planned economy's dangers. In the 1980s, governments worldwide made reforms that encouraged private investment, an end to price controls, and lower tax rates. Along the way, the tide turned, and the Austrians' free-market ideas took a back seat to Keynesian economics. Consequently, debt levels have climbed dramatically across the developed world.

Hayek warned us of tyranny's danger that inevitably results from centralized planning. He reasoned that tyranny is the inevitable result of government policies aimed at preventing market competition. As long as voters demand that government protect them from negative economic change, governments can oblige them only by eliminating competition, entrepreneurship, innovation, and consumer sovereignty. According to Hayek, global prosperity requires real change—and that change is impossible without some people suffering distress.

The road that ultimately leads to the loss of personal freedom is centralized planning. Planners tend to become fixated on achieving their specified goals on specified dates regardless of the facts. The loss of personal freedom comes when planners realize that the only way to achieve these goals is to mandate that everyone adhere to the plan. Thus the road to serfdom is complete. At this point, growth policies are wholly subservient to the policies of planners. We are witnessing this with the government's response to the pandemic in 2021; growth policies are put on the back burner while governments shut down their economies.

How do we best solve our economic problems? Keynesian economists would argue that the problem is economical and that we need to pull the right levers to revive the economy. Austrian economists argue that our issues are more political than economic. If the crises were economic, they argue, we could reduce corporate tax rates and red tape to encourage investment and risk-taking. Instead, European and American policymakers have pursued every possible fix, except Austrian policies, to avoid addressing the core problems because people have accepted an entitlement mentality. According to the book, *The 4% Solution*, most Americans receive some form of government assistance, causing a big increase in the national debt. Habits of dependency, as any addict knows, are difficult to change.

Basic economics teaches us that growth stems from savings and investment. But the artificially low interest rates perpetuated by monetary policies discourage savings, and lengthy and confusing laws stifle investments; thus, the economy stagnates with a reduction in savings and investing. According to Austrian economics, we should implement policies that encourage saving and investment. We need rules and regulations and a tax system that will encourage growth. Incredibly, few world leaders support pro-growth policies. The author claims that if we can grow 4% annually, we can solve our problems. Because newscasters can skew the news to fit their view of the world, a basic understanding of economics is important if we are going to protect our freedom and prosperity.

Do government policies, taxes, programs, and regulations, promote economic growth and protect individual liberties or do they inhibit growth and diminish personal freedoms? We can raise wages, clean the environment, achieve full-employment, pursue clean energy sources, and protect individual rights, but only if we sufficiently grow. But if our laws and policies lead to a shrinkage of the economic pie, the result will be inflation and unemployment.

In the book *Endgame: The End of The Debt Super Cycle And How It Changes Everything*, John Mauldin states:

> *There are only two ways that you can grow the economy. You can either increase your working-age population or increase productivity. There is no magic fairy dust to grow the economy. To increase GDP, you actually have to produce something.*

Full- Employment

The labor force consists of employed persons and persons who are actively seeking gainful employment. A person has to be seeking gainful employment to be considered unemployed. We cannot have zero percent unemployment because someone is always seeking employment, the largest group being recent high school and college graduates. The Bureau of Labor Statistics considers the economy to be fully employed if four to six percent of the labor force is seeking gainful employment.

The Full- Employment Act of 1946 mandates the federal government to predict the next fiscal year's employment rate. Congress must submit full-employment policies if the projected rate is less than full-employment. Austrian economists have objections to the act for the following reasons:

■ Business cycles are natural, and therefore we should allow them to run their course without allowing federal mandates to cause disruptions.

■ Economists identify three time lags: recognition, decision, and action lag. The recognition lag is the time it take to recognize we have a problem; the decision lag is the time it takes to make decisions; and the action lag is the time it takes to implement policies. Because of time lags, once government policy is implemented, the situation may be different. Consequently, government policies tend to be pro-cyclical rather than counter-cyclical, meaning they can accentuate the business cycle's ups and downs instead of smoothing them out.

■ Forecasting future activity can be difficult, if not impossible.

The Employment Act of 1946 stipulated economic goals, but it did not ask the Fed to manage the economy. The mandate to manage the economy came with the Full- Employment and Balanced Growth Act of 1978, also known as the Humphrey-Hawkins Full- Employment Act. This act mandated the Federal Reserve to ensure both price stability and full-employment. The remedy to cure inflation is to reduce the money supply and the solution to cure unemployment is to increase the money supply; the Fed cannot simultaneously fight both problems.

At times, the Fed has admitted that its policies were counterproductive, but the law forced it to do something, anything, to satisfy the law's mandates. The Fed is effective at fighting inflation because people have no choice but to spend less when it decreases the money supply. But the Fed cannot force people to spend money, limiting its usefulness when unemployment is the problem. Austrian economists favor ending this dual mandate and thereby liberating the central bank to focus on stabilizing prices.

Stable Prices

Economists define inflation as an increase in the average price level. A small amount of inflation is not harmful, especially if people predict it, and it occurs regularly. However, inflation can cause problems if it exceeds five percent a year and is unpredictable. Inflation diminishes consumers' buying power as prices rise more than incomes, thus pushing the economy into recession.

Efficiency

Economists describe an increase in productivity as producing more with less or when outputs exceed inputs. When businesses increase productivity, there is an incentive to lower prices because producers want to increase their market share. Sam Walton made Wal-Mart a success with low costs and low prices, squashing the competition in the process. Because Wal-Mart is so efficient, it has provided jobs for a large portion of America's workforce.

CHAPTER 2: DECISIONS

The U.S. Constitution gave Congress the power of the purse as a check against excessive Executive overreach. However, in 2010 President Obama decreed by executive order the Consumer Financial Protection Bureau. The CFPB is an independent entity that has authority over the financial sector. The Federal Reserve houses this agency, finances this agency-but it does not control it. Austrian economists would argue that this agency is unconstitutional and violates the rule of law because when government agencies pass judgment beyond elective officials' scope, citizens have no recourse.

The Consumer Financial Protection Bureau uses the concept of disparate impact to assess financial institutions. Disparate impact holds that we may consider employment practices unfair and illegal if they have a disproportionate "adverse impact" on members of a minority group. Under the doctrine, the government can punish a firm if its practices have a disproportionately adverse effect on members of a protected class of people than non-members of the protected class. In other words, authorities can penalize a business even though no one brings a discrimination charge against it. If the employee makeup does not adhere to the racial or ethnic mix that the CFBP mandates, the CFBP penalizes the firm for discrimination. Disparate impact hurts economic efficiency because its actions can be arbitrary. Businesses have no way of knowing before the fact if they violate the law. Thus, the application of disparate impact breeds uncertainty and diminishes investment and growth.

Fairness

People still come to America seeking opportunity because they believe the system is fair and rewards risk taking and hard work. But the concept of fairness and equity can relative. Is it fair that some people have more money than other people? Would not an even distribution of income be the most equitable situation? If we had an even distribution of income, where would the incentive to take risks come from? When investments are insufficient to grow the economy, the government will take up the slack, extinguishing all personal freedom.

Consider what happened in Europe. For many years, the countries in Europe built such large and expensive social programs that almost everyone became recipients of government programs. Eventually, Europe neglected pro-growth policies in favor of income redistribution policies to the point that their economies shrank, forcing countries to go deep into debt. Excessive debt and slow growth led to downgrades in their credit ratings, and as their credit dried up, stronger nations, like Germany, had to bail them out.

Minimize Pollution

A weakness of a free market system is that it cannot guarantee safe working conditions and a clean environment. Unsafe working conditions and pollution are examples of negative externalities, the unpleasant by-products of the industrial process. Consider the following. Suppose company A cares about pollution and safety issues and invests in safe machines and anti-pollution devices. Consequently, its costs rise, its ability to compete diminishes, and eventually it goes out of business. The only solution is for the federal government to pass laws that require all companies to establish environmentally sound practices. In this way, companies can compete on a level playing field. The challenge is to promote a safe and clean environment without sabotaging the economy, mainly because of foreign competition.

Economists agree that federal regulations are necessary for a clean environment, but economists and politicians disagree over the specifics. The debate has long existed over the effectiveness and fairness of the U.S. Environmental Protection Agency. Traditionally, the EPA has evaluated regulatory initiatives from a scientific perspective first, an economic outlook second, a legal perspective third, and political considerations. Today political ambitions come first, legal perspectives second, technical perspectives third, and economic perspectives a distant fourth. In the recent past, regulations were developed and implemented concerning the administration's political whims. These overzealous actions of the EPA stand a chance to undermine and weaken the economy.

Security

All of us are dependent on a healthy economy because the government cannot create jobs, guarantee growth, or establish security; governments can only redistribute what the economy produces. If the economy grows less, society receives less. The more government forces regulations and taxes on productive people, the more obstacles to a healthy and productive economy. When the financial panic hit in 2008, the EU and International

Monetary Fund urged governments across the Continent to spend like crazy to avoid recession. So they spent, only to discover that such spending is unsustainable.

FREEDOM AND THE NATIONAL DEBT

The federal government borrows money by selling bonds, which we call securities. A bond is an agreement between a borrower and a lender regarding the amount, the interest rate, and the maturity date. The deficit is yearly and the debt is the total amount of indebtedness. Excessive debt can lead to a loss of economic freedom as more and more of the country's resources go to funding the debt. A trillion dollars in $100 bills would weigh 22 million pounds! If you stack one hundred dollar bills on top of each other, you would penetrate the Earth's atmosphere and keep on going—678 miles high. A trillion is a million million. The national debt clock on the internet https://usdebtclock.org/ gives facts about the U.S. National Debt. The federal government has run deficits for all but a few years since 1945. The deficit is the amount of money government borrows each year and debt is the total owed.

David Walker, the previous head of the U.S. Government Accountability Office (GAO), used to travel the United States warning people of the dangers of America's debt burden. He tells anyone who will listen that the U.S. debt economy is unsustainable. He believes that fiscal policies have resulted in an economic tsunami and leave little time to change course. Since the American dollar is the world's standard currency and interest rates are low, we have managed this massive debt. But the dollar will eventually fail to the world's standard currency and interest rates will rise.

What is the difference between private and government debt? Children are not responsible for the obligations of their parents. But the younger generation will find themselves responsible for dealing with the enormous debt left to it by their parents and grandparents. Keynesians believe that by raising taxes on the top income earners, we can afford our social programs, fund the military, and pay off the national debt. Keynesians believe that because the rich have so much money, this increase in taxes will not diminish investments or stifle growth. Austrian economists believe that we should stimulate growth by lowering taxes and lessening regulations, especially on business groups.

SUMMARY

A free enterprise system uses the price mechanism to transmit information, give incentives, and promote investments. Free enterprise needs a strong central government to enforce laws. Fair laws favor order and growth; bad laws favor disorder and stagnation. Good governments promote a healthy distribution of income and help reduce negative externalities, such as pollution and unsafe working conditions.

We need to modify the free market system, but if the government interferes too much and wrongly, price signals blur, and incentives are impaired. Consequently, we experience more inflation, an increase in unemployment, a decline in living standards, a general breakdown of the economic and political systems, and perhaps more violence.

When the federal government becomes too large and intrusive, it can be detrimental to our freedom and security. Through the practice of rent-seeking, companies can unduly influence legislation to their benefit. When political favoritism becomes the norm, moral hazards can eventually destroy our free market system.

America is a democracy in a republic, which means that most voters influence legislation, but we have laws that help protect the minority from the majority. When most voters are net receivers of the government largess, the majority can take everything away from the minority. When the minority represents business owners and entrepreneurs, the system, as we know it, collapses.

CHAPTER 3
GROWTH

Adam Smith, in his book, *An Inquiry into the Nature and Causes of the Wealth of Nations*, 1776, described the efficiency of market economies. In the first chapter, 'Of the Division of Labour,' he describes how society raises its standard of living by increasing productivity. How can the standard of living be high in the United States and low in many other countries? A part of the answer is a difference in natural resources, but not entirely. For example, Pakistan and Bangladesh are underdeveloped countries with an abundance of suitable soil and water. Simultaneously, the countries of Japan and Switzerland lack natural resources yet have a high standard of living.

STANDARD OF LIVING

Economists define a country's standard of living as the minimum necessities and luxuries of life to which a person or a group may be accustomed to or aspire. A country's standard of living will increase when society saves and then uses the savings to make profitable investments. World War 2 all but destroyed Japan's economy. So its leaders passed laws that encouraged people to save. Then leaders passed laws encouraging business people to borrow the savings to make investments, which grew the economy. Some people look at Japan's growth as a miracle, but the growth resulted from saving and investing. Notice also that Japan encouraged its citizens to save; it did not have to borrow from foreign countries.

However, the Japanese could have built a more robust economy had they supported the most creditworthy people instead of lending money to friends, family, and people who offered the highest bribes. This favoritism led to unsound investments, bankruptcy, and government bailouts. Only through robust growth can society prosper. When we give growth a low priority, practice favoritism, and neglect the rule of law, the market falters.

During the 1920s, about 25 percent of America's population lived on working farms, compared to about 3 percent today. Large farms have made it possible for farmers to invest in efficient tractors, machinery, modern technology, fertilizers, and pesticides. The American farmer is the most efficient in the world. The downside to large farms is the concentration of power. For example, Bill Gates is the largest owner of farmland in the United States. Another example of an increase in productivity is the light bulb. Thomas Edison invented the first electric lamp in 1879. In those early days, four glassblowers could make twelve hundred bulbs a day, and by 1926, workers could produce two thousand bulbs per minute. Today, each operated by only one person, fourteen glassblowing machines make about 90 percent of all the light bulbs used in the United States. In 1900, the average American had to work a full day to buy one light bulb; today, they are cheap. Notice that growth is a two-step process; first, we must save, and second, we must invest in ways that will increase productivity and grow the economy.

The Rule of Law

Secure property rights are essential to a prosperous free economy, but these rights can be fragile. For example, when Zimbabwe won its independence from Great Britain in 1980, it was one of Africa's most prosperous nations. Soon after taking power, President Robert Mugabe began disassembling the rule of law, eventually confiscating all property rights while controlling prices. Consequently, unemployment ensued, investments languished, and inflation skyrocketed, causing mass shortages of almost everything.

When the federal government bailed out General Motors in 2009, it ignored current bankruptcy laws and picked the winners and losers. The government paid auto unions full because of their generous political contributions but short-changed bondholders and the non-union members at Delphi, GM's former subsidiary. Delphi, which underwent the most protracted corporate bankruptcy in U.S. history, lost all of its health and life insurance benefits, and 70,000 retirees lost as much as 65% of their benefits.

Businesses will make investments if they are confident about the rules of the game and anticipate profit. Unlike the government, business people have to make profits. When government intervenes with market forces and makes decisions on an ad-hoc basis, it introduces an element of uncertainty into the mix, diminishing investments and stifling growth; investors will not make investments with doubt and fear in their hearts.

Taxes and Regulations

Most citizens do not mind paying reasonable taxes and adhering to sensible laws and regulations; we all see the benefit in driving on the same side of the road or knowing what is in the food we eat. A marginal tax rate of 15 percent will not encourage tax evasion, but beyond some point, increases in marginal tax rates will lead to increases in unreported income.

European nations impose excessive regulations on businesses, especially Greece, France, Spain, and Italy, making it difficult, and in some cases impossible, to fire anyone. The amount of paperwork and legal proceedings that an employer has to undertake to get rid of an employee are intimidating. There is even a particular judicial system in France for dismissed workers whereby employers lose the legal battles more than 75 percent of the time. Consequently, businesses seek out workers who agree to accept cash payments and are willing to work without a contract.

History has taught us that countries will eventually stagnate that ignore the rule of law, impose high taxes and excessive regulations, and have a high national debt. On the other hand, countries that pass reasonable pro-growth laws, respect the rule of law, and have a small national debt grow. There will always be fluctuations in economic activity; there will always be ups and downs with winners and losers, and there will always be an uneven distribution of wealth. We can overlook these negative aspects of a free market as long as there is upward mobility.

Part-Time Work

When the U.S. Congress passed the Affordable Care Act

in 2010, referred to as ObamaCare, health care changed. Some businesses only hire part-time workers who work less than 30 hours a week to avoid the law's mandates. The Internal Revenue Code defines part-time employees as those who work 1,000 hours or less in any 12-month period, which equivocates 30 hours a week. Federal laws consider full-time employees with full benefits as covered employees and part-time employees without benefits as non-covered. Because of the added costs imposed on businesses for health care, there has been an increase in non-covered employment and a reduction in covered jobs.

PRODUCTIVITY

Most everyone benefits when businesses find ways to reduce costs and prices. The business gains with higher profits, and the consumer gains with lower prices. The economy gains because of robust growth, and the government gains because of higher tax revenues. Most everyone loses when costs increase. When costs increase, businesses who face an elastic demand curve tend to go out of business, and companies that face a demand curve that is more inelastic raise their prices. In both cases, there is a decrease in aggregate demand leading to unemployment.

Henry Ford walked into his office one day in 1914 and announced that he would double his worker's wages to $5 a day. The year before, Ford had revolutionized manufacturing with the moving assembly line, slashing automobile build times to just 90 minutes from 14 hours, allowing him to reduce his cars' price while underpricing 88 competitors. Productivity gains like these transform lifestyles and cause nations to prosper. Other inventions are the telephone in 1876, phonograph 1877, motion pictures 1893, airplanes 1903, radio 1920, television 1945, and the iPad in 2009.

Inventions

Is the following statement true or false? If a tractor can do the job of 100 workers, it is taking the jobs of 100 workers. The statement is false. The truth is that if it were not for the tractor, no one would have a job. Consider the following story. Peter wants land plowed for a garden. Matthew, a neighbor who has a tractor and a plow, agrees to plow his land, which will take about an hour, for $25. When Peter needs his land plowed the next year, he contacts Matthew again. This time, however, Matthew says, *I would be pleased to plow your field, but I no longer have a tractor. But I can plow it with a rake and shovel, which will take about ten hours, for $25 an hour.* Now Peter considers that he could buy a whole lot of vegetables for $250. He says to his neighbor, *Last year, I paid you by the job, not by the hour. If you plow my garden by hand, I will still give you $25.* Being no fool, Matthew declines the offer. So, you see, without the tractor there would be no job.

Automation

Joe lost his job after working at the local factory for twenty years because his company purchased new machines and terminated 100 people. It would not be easy to convince Joe that automation generates more jobs than it replaces. This factory has fired workers, but it is also true that automation creates more jobs than it displaces. When businesses increase productivity, they can reduce their prices, which increases consumer's real incomes and increase demand. Lost jobs are mostly unskilled labor-intensive jobs, and the ones gained are the higher-skill type jobs. Companies are continually searching for skilled workers, and when they cannot find them here, they explore the foreign market.

Freedom

More than 150 years ago, the French nobleman Alexis de Tocqueville toured America and pondered why America was more successful than other countries. He concluded that America was prosperous because we believed in upward mobility and that the future will be better than the present and people believed that we may be poor today, but if we can be rich tomorrow.

Horatio Alger (1832-1899) influenced America by writing stories about boys who would claw their way out of poverty to prosperity. A classic tale was about a poor boy who, while walking to school barefooted, has a dream in his heart and a steadfast desire to succeed. Horatio Alger's stories lit a fire in the hearts and minds of a whole generation of Americans who rose from poverty and built successful businesses.

When individuals work and invest, the economy grows and prospers; when the government imposes excessive taxes and regulations, the economy suffers. An example of this is what happened in Germany after World War II. Between 1945 and 1947, Germany experienced extreme price controls and a restrictive economy. In 1948, when Ludwig Erhard lifted price controls and advocated a free market economy, the nation prospered.

WHY PRODUCTIVITY DECLINES

Trade Restrictions

Economies of large-scale operation can be more efficient than small scale operations. When production increases, companies can find more ways to divide the labor, use by-products, employ robotics, and buy raw materials at lower prices, thus lowering costs. International trade can increase economies of scale and benefit all countries. However, trade restrictions limit the advantages of commerce. The collective always favors free trade, but individual countries favor trade restrictions.

For example, in 2010, Brazil sued America for unfair and unlawful trade practices. America was subsidizing cotton farmers, a powerful special interest group, enabling them to sell their cotton for less than the Brazilians. The World Trade Organization ruled that subsidies to American cotton growers under the 2008 farm bill violate U.S. trading commitments. The U.S. lost its final appeal in the case, and the WTO gave Brazil the right to retaliate. Brazil dropped the suit when the U.S. Congress agreed to subsidize Brazilian cotton growers!

Anti-Pollution & Consumer Safety Laws

There are problems that only government can fix and the free market cannot fix. For example, businesses left on their own do not have an incentive to curb pollution. If a business owner has a social conscience and invests in anti-pollution devices, its costs and prices would have to increase, thus diminishing its ability to compete. Knowing that competitors will not follow suit, the business decides not to follow its social conscience, and therefore society experiences excessive pollution.

The solution to this problem is for the government to enforce environmental regulations on all businesses. But what happens when the restrictions are too harsh? What happens when policymakers ignore economic growth? Government policies can hinder productivity by raising costs, entangling businesses in excessive regulations, and fostering an environment of doubt and fear. Companies may be reluctant to invest for fear of government policies and policies not yet on the books.

Consider the Environmental Protection Agency's (EPA) campaign against coal. Coal-fired plants currently provide power to the population. The EPA forces many coal-fired power plants to shut down because it supports alternative energy sources like solar power, natural gas, and wind power. You should ask yourself who these people are with so much power to make decisions that affect everyone. Do they have an understanding of economics, or are they fanatics? Are they making decisions based on economics or politics?

Taxes

No one disputes that society needs to pay taxes to fund such things as public goods, including parks, roads, and schools. But when the government imposes excessive regulations and taxes on businesses, investments and efficiency decline. There is a moral question of how far the government can go imposing its will on citizens. Does the government grant privilege to its citizens, or do citizens have natural rights? The US Constitution states that citizens have natural rights.

Government Policies Trump the Market

Programs such as the Community Reinvestment Act and the Federal Reserve's zero interest rate policy (ZIRP) have impacted the economy. The government imposed "affordable housing" requirements on Fannie Mae and Freddie Mac in 1992 when it passed the Community Reinvestment Act. Fannie Mae and Freddie Mac do not lend money; they buy mortgages from lending institutions. Before 1992, the government required Fannie Mae and Freddie Mac to buy only prime mortgages. After 1992, Congress required Fannie and Freddie to meet government quotas when they bought loans from banks and other mortgage originators.

Years ago, banks would keep loans in house and collect monthly payments. Today banks sell the loans to Fannie Mae and Freddie Mac, and other financial institutions who bundle the loans into individual securities, called asset-backed securities, with different levels of risk and rates of return. The loans can be commercial, student loans, or mortgages. The Federal Reserve, in 2012, announced it would stimulate the US economy by purchasing mortgage-backed securities and government bonds with newly created money, something economists call 'monetizing the debt' or 'quantitative easing.' These purchases increase the money supply, which puts downward pressure on interest rates. However, the lower interest rates punish savers.

Trouble begins whenever companies spend less on research and development and more on rent-seeking. This partnership between big business and government is a destructive force, undermining the economy and political system. Rent-seeking allows the government to pick the winners and losers. Economists call this crony capitalism.

Debt Discourages Productivity

With a national debt exceeding thirty-trillion dollars, the government uses much of its resources to repay the debt to the world bankers. The prime interest rate, the lowest interest rate that banks charge their most credit-worthy customers, was 21 percent in 1980. With a national debt of thirty trillion dollars, what would happen to our economy with rising interest rates?

OVER REGULATION AND PRODUCTIVITY

In some cities, kids cannot open a lemonade stand without a permit. A town in California disallowed a young girl to sell mistletoe to buy braces but allowed her to beg for money. These policies stifle entrepreneurship.

Sarbanes-Oxley

Congress passed the Sarbanes-Oxley Accounting Reform Act in 2002, giving the government more power to intervene in credit markets. The danger is that the bill has given the government a tool to impose penalties on selected companies. Sarbanes-Oxley established the Public Company Accounting Oversight Board and mandated internal management reports showing how well the company is following the board's dictates. Section 404 requires costly external audits of companies, apart from a company's financial statements. Sarbanes - Oxley is the most apparent sign of over-regulation and the primary reason foreign companies forgo U.S. public listing. Larger firms support the law because they can absorb the high costs of compliance, whereas smaller firms fall by the wayside.

No Child Left Behind Act (NCLB)

Rachel Carson Middle School in Herndon, Virginia, is full of winners. The school won a governor's award for teaching excellence from 2007 to 2011, and the national forum for middle-school improvement cited Rachel Carson as a school to watch. Yet, the federal government considers Rachel Carson a failing school, although the school has high average scores. The government has designed the law to highlight achievements according to race, gender, and income. Consequently, the government can declare high-performing schools failures.

Patient Protection & Affordable Care Act

The Patient Protection and Affordable Care Act (PPACA), also called Affordable Care Act (ACA), or Obamacare, was signed into law in 2010. Who knew what was in the 2,700-page health bill before Congress passed it? Even Nancy Pelosi, Speaker of the House, admitted she did not know everything in the bill. Bills like these have fostered an atmosphere of uncertainty and fear, which erodes investments, economic growth and diminishes productivity.

Wall Street Protection Act

President Obama signed into law the 2,300-page Financial Reform Bill in 2010, also known as the Dodd-Frank Law or Wall Street Reform and Consumer Protection Act. Among other things, the law provides incentives to encourage banking for low and moderate-income individuals. It gives government the authority to liquidate failing financial institutions. The law also expanded the Federal Reserve's regulatory powers, established the Consumer Financial Protection Bureau, and enhanced the Securities and Exchange Commission's authority. The Dodd-Frank Law is an example of the excessive regulation that hampers productivity gains.

The federal government and much of the financial system could not function without private accounting firms such as Promontory, Deloitte, PricewaterhouseCoopers, and Ernst & Young. Regulators and banks hire firms to investigate suspicious activity, act as intermediaries between government and private companies and advise financial institutions on how to comply with complex regulatory rules. Consultants have become so crucial to the system that they help shape it. Promontory is arguably the most powerful of these regulators and can receive up to $1,500 an hour for its services. This is a huge expense for companies trying to meet government mandates.

The Financial Stability Oversight Council (FSOC) and the Consumer Financial Protection Bureau (CFPB) have absolute power. The FSOC can declare a financial firm systemically important based on any risk-related factors that it deems appropriate. The CFPB can punish responsible lenders who offer loans that the bureau later believes to be 'unfair,' 'deceptive,' or '"abusive.'

The Constitution empowers the President, Congress, and the courts to prevent regulators from running amok with excessive, arbitrary, or discriminatory regulations. However, Dodd-Frank does not honor checks and balances; it eliminates them. The CFPB is not subject to Congress's 'power of the purse,' which James Madison knew to be Congress's 'most complete and effectual weapon.' Instead, Dodd-Frank lets the CFPB demand millions annually from the Federal Reserve and prohibits Congress from reviewing its budget. The president has limited authority over the CFPB.

The Financial Stability Oversight Council is free from checks and balances. For example, when the Council—a working group of the Treasury secretary, Federal Reserve chairman, comptroller of the currency, and other unelected regulators—deems a financial institution too big to fail, the FSOC prohibits the courts from reviewing whether the regulators correctly interpreted the law.

When the FSOC declares that a corporation is systemically important—that its failure poses a threat to US financial stability—the government is effectively saying that it will do whatever it takes to prevent the firm from failing. Thus, it gives a market advantage to large firms over small firms. Consequently, the American economy will move toward ever-larger firms, reducing competition.

The Consumer Financial Protection Bureau and the Financial Stability Oversight Council's constitutional violations are not merely the stuff of law-school debates; they pose a direct threat to economic recovery. Community banks are afraid of lending money because the CFPB might later decide that the loans were unfair. American finance is becoming more political, less vibrant, and further removed from the rule-of-law principles. Regulators can take over a struggling bank and every affiliate in the bank's network by merely claiming that it is in danger of default. Once an institution falls into the government's hands, the FDIC can choose whom to pay and how much. An example of this is what happened in 2009 when the government bailed out Chrysler and gave unions preferential treatment over bondholders, an act that adds a layer of confusion and because it is contrary to bankruptcy law.

SUMMARY

Keynesian economists favor a more intrusive government than do Austrians. Keynesians support income distribution policies more so than Austrians. Austrians believe that there will always be income inequality because of differences in risk tolerance, the way people value leisure time and creativity.

We live well only if we produce well, and we produce well only if we save and make wise investments. Growth is the key to economic well-being, and growth is a direct result of increasing productivity. Lower costs lead to lower prices, more growth, and a higher standard of living for most people. Thus, most everyone gains. When productivity declines and things wear out over time, costs increase, prices rise, consumers buy less, and the economy stagnates.

A free market can only maintain its vitality if we let the losers lose and the winners win. The economic system does this by rewarding sound business ventures and allowing unsound business ventures to fail. Participants in the economy need clear and precise rules. Everything else being equal, this process leads to a growing and robust economy.

Let's assume you own a business, and you have one million dollars to invest. Should you invest the money, or should you hire lobbyists? You are practicing rent-seeking if you decide to put money into Washington, D.C. Moral hazard occurs when the government supports failing companies.

CHAPTER 4
DEMAND & SUPPLY

A good is scarce when it is not readily available to everyone. Usefulness and scarcity determine the market value of goods and services as portrayed by demand and supply curves. The demand curve is a visual representation of the quantity of a good or service consumers will purchase at each possible price. It plots the relationship between quantity and price consumers will buy at different prices. A supply curve is a graph showing the amount of a good or service producers offer at various prices during a specific time. A company's supply curve illustrates the number of goods and services the company is willing to supply at every possible price.

The equilibrium price is the only price where consumers' desires and the desires of producers agree—that is, where the amount of the product that consumers want to buy (quantity demanded) is equal to the amount producers want to sell (quantity supplied). This mutually desired amount is called the equilibrium quantity. Demand and supply curves together determine the equilibrium price and, eventually, and after time lags, the market price. The equilibrium price changes when demand and supply curves shift because the equilibrium price is the price toward which the economy tends.

DEMAND CURVES

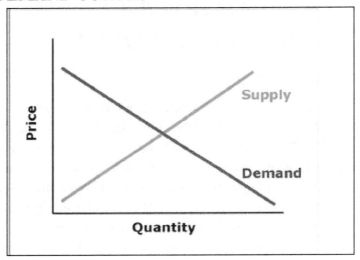

The demand curve measures the level of consumer desires for goods and services. A demand curve is a graphical illustration of the relationship between the price of a good, shown on the vertical axis, and the quantity of that good demanded, shown on the horizontal axis. We are assuming that nothing else changes when price changes; therefore, as the price of a good decrease, consumers will buy more, and as the price increases, they will buy less. Thus, a demand curve shows an inverse relationship between price and quantity.

WHY DEMAND CURVES SHIFT:
Real Incomes

When economists consider income, they always mean real income: persons, buying power considering a change in prices—real income increases when money income exceeds the general price level. Therefore, the consumer can afford to buy more goods and services when their real income increases and less when their real income decreases. When economists refer to income, they always mean real income, unless otherwise stated.

Normal goods are goods that consumers buy more of as their incomes increase. Assuming that iPads are normal goods, consumers will buy more of them as their incomes rise, an increase in consumer income will shift demand from D1 to D2. The demand curve for iPads will shift to the left when consumer income decreases.

An inferior good is a good that consumers will purchase less of as their incomes rise. When consumer income increases, people tend to buy more new cars and fewer used cars. Therefore, new vehicles is an example of a normal good, and used cars is an example of an inferior good. Again, the demand curve for normal goods will increase when consumer income increase and the demand for inferior goods will decrease as income increases.

Tastes and Preferences

Consumers' tastes and preferences are always changing. The demand curve will shift to the right when consumer desire for iPads increases to the left when it decreases. This change in demand may result from a new invention, marketing, or an event, such as a recession.

Price of Related Products

If the price of comparable products change, such as competing tablets, the demand curve for iPads will reflect the change. If prices of competing tablets increase, the demand for iPads will increase and vice versa. A price change causes a movement along the curve, but the whole curve shifts if the price of competing goods (either substitutes or complements) change.

Two goods are substitutes for each other if an increase in the price of one causes consumers to buy more of the other. If the price of lettuce increases while the price of cabbage stays the same, consumers will buy more cabbage and less lettuce because lettuce and cabbage are substitutes for one another.

Two goods are complements to one another when an increase (decrease) in demand for one good causes an increase (decrease) in demand for the other. If shrimp's price increases, the quantity demanded will decrease, and the demand for shrimp sauce will decrease because of the relationship between shrimp and shrimp sauce. Notice that for shrimp, there is a change in the quantity demanded, a movement along the demand curve, but for shrimp sauce, the whole curve is shifts.

Market Size

As more people enter the market, there is a tendency for demand to increase for every good and service. A supermarket full of people will tend to sell more food than a market with few customers. Why will a restaurant build next to a competing restaurant? Or, why would an O'Reilly Auto Parts Store build a store next to an existing Advance Auto Parts Store? Businesses are more successful when they are grouped instead of by themselves. Everyone gains from a robust traffic flow in a central location; everyone gains when the market is large compared to the small market size. This explains the advantage of international trade.

Expectations

A change in expectation can cause demand curves to shift because we tend to make decisions based on what we expect to happen in the future. If you think it will be cold, you will wear a coat; if you think it will be hot, you wear shorts. Advertising can change your perception of a product; expectations can affect a change in demand for a product. If consumers believe that sugar's price was about to increase a lot, they will tend to purchase more sugar in anticipation of the higher price in the future. Notice that the price of sugar did not change—consumer expectations changed.

Life can be a self-fulfilling prophecy; whatever we expect to happen tends to happen. If we expect a shortage, we tend to purchase more of that good or service. This increase in demand will cause a shortage, just what we expected to happen. Notice that this can be a self-fulfilling prophecy. If enough potential consumers expect the price of houses to increase, they will tend to buy now instead of waiting. This increase in demand will increase the price of houses.

THE UPWARD SLOPING SUPPLY CURVE

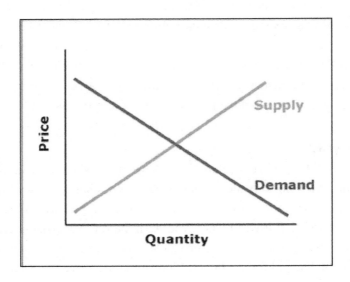

Supply curves represent suppliers of a good or service. For example, you and other college students are the potential suppliers of labor. If the wage for computer programmers increase and the salary for social workers decrease, more students will choose the computer field over social work; there will be an increase in the quantity supplied as price (wage) increases and a decrease in the amount provided as the price (wage) decreases. There are two explanations for this direct relationship between price and quantity for a good or service: why is it that when the market price of good increases, the amount supplied will also increase and vise versa?

■ Businesses may experience an increase in costs as the quantity supplied increases. When this happens, suppliers will have an incentive to increase the amount supplied if they receive a price increase. The price increase must be enough to cover the increased cost of producing the additional units.

■ Incentives will change as the market dictates higher prices. As prices increase, suppliers can make more money and greater profits, and therefore they have an incentive to increase the quantity supplied. How do we know this will happen? When the price changes, we assume that nothing else changes.

Economists always assume that costs (what suppliers pay to supply something) do not change when the price changes (what they charge for the good or service in the market place). We always make the other things being equal assumption. We always assume that nothing else changes when the price changes. If we did make this assumption, then we could not come to a definitive conclusion as to what would happen when the price changes. If the price decreases, the supplier makes less money, and therefore the quantity supplied decreases because the supplier has less incentive to supply at the lower price. If the price increases, the supplier will make more profit, again, because we assume that the only thing changing here is the price, not costs, nothing.

SUPPLY CURVE SHIFTS

We witness a shift in supply curves when we relax the all else being equal assumption. When something changes that influence the supply for a good or service, other than the price, the whole curve will shift. Cost is the sum of payments made by an enterprise to production factors, such as raw materials, labor, utilities, and maintenance. Cost of production (not the price of the product) is the most decisive factor, affecting a shift in supply curves. When costs rise, the supply curve will shift to the left; as costs decrease, the supply curve will shift to the right. If you were a cattle farmer, you would tend to purchase more fertilizer if the price of fertilizer decreased, and your grass would grow faster, and you could raise more cattle on the same amount of land as before; supply has increased. Thus, when your costs decrease, the supply of livestock will increase, and vice versa.

Economists make a distinction between the short run and the long run. A business can increase or decrease production, but it cannot change its plant capacity in the short run. Once a company changes its plant capacity by expanding or contracting, we are in the long run. In the short run, there is always an optimal factory production level, whereby a certain level of production will produce the most efficient use of its inputs. Costs will decrease as output increases to this most efficient output level; an increase in output beyond this level will increase costs. A business can grow by making additions to the existing plant or building new plants in the long run.

Production costs can be affected by workers' wages, raw materials, transportation, energy, and taxes. If there is a change in these costs or any other costs, the supply curve will shift. Consider what happens when the price of oil increases – this tends to increase the cost of chemical fertilizers. The higher production cost will cause the supply curve for fertilizer to shift to the left; a reduction in costs would shift the supply curve to the right. Improvements in technology have lowered the cost of computers, resulting in more computers supplied at different prices. Other factors that cause supply curves to shift are:

- Changes in technology.
- Costs of relevant resources.
- Prices of alternative goods.
- Producer expectations.

Technology

A technology change can lead to improvements of an existing product or the development of a new one. When Microsoft came out with a tablet PC in 1999; they were not popular because they were too heavy to hold with one hand, did not have a virtual keyboard, and lacked applications. When Apple Computer came out with the first iPad in 2010, it ushered in a new phase. Experts thought that tablets would never sell because people had computers.

Resources

All businesses have to use resources that are relevant to their business. For example, hay is a relevant resource for a cattle rancher, but not for a coffee shop owner. A change in hay price will affect the cattle farmer but not affect the coffee shop owner. If the coffee beans price increases, the cattle rancher is not affected, but the coffee shop owner is affected.

Alternative Goods

What should you plant if you own a produce farm? You have a choice of vegetables; each vegetable is an alternative product for all the others. Suppose you grow cabbage. Then, the government mandates more ethanol gasoline. This mandate will increase corn's market price, giving you an incentive to grow corn.

Expectations

Suppliers' expectation is a powerful force because suppliers decide based on what they think will happen in the future.

MARKET EQUILIBRIUM

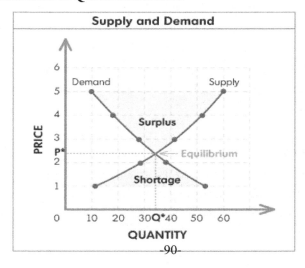

The market answers the three questions of what, how much, and for whom to produce. Market equilibrium is the point at which the demand and supply curve intersect, where there is an agreement on price between the buyer and the seller. There is no shortage or surplus at the equilibrium point; the price clears the market, and the quantity supplied equals quantity demanded.

Why is the intersection of demand and supply an equilibrium? There will be a surplus above this price, and suppliers will lower the price to eliminate the surplus; below this price, there will be a shortage, and suppliers sell to the highest bidder. Economists define the equilibrium price as the price toward which the economy tends. Keep in mind that life is always a flow situation. Things do not come to an abrupt halt and then stop. When certain variables change, demand and supply curves shift, equilibrium changes, and markets adjust. Thus the equilibrium is the point toward which the economy tends.

MARKETS

Suppose the market is in disequilibrium, which means it is not at the equilibrium. As the market moves toward equilibrium, it will not stop abruptly when it gets to the equilibrium point. It will flow past it to another disequilibrium point, at which time it will change course and start heading back toward equilibrium again. Because this is a never-ending cycle, the equilibrium is the point toward which the economy tends, not the point at which it stays.

The swiftness or slowness of these adjustments depends on the market. In a market where many buyers and sellers have no control over the price and where everyone knows the facts and government policies do not impede market forces, any adjustments will be swift. An excessive quantity demanded or excessive quantity supplied will quickly put upward or downward pressure on prices. The more impediments there are to this process, the slower the adjustments and the longer it will take the market to regain equilibrium.

Technology has made adjustments quicker and more fluid than ever before. Consider Mary Smith, a 25-year-old college student who walked into Best Buy in Christiansburg, Virginia, and spotted her husband's perfect gift. Last year, she might have just dropped the $184.85 Garmin global positioning system into her cart. This time, she took out her phone and typed the model number into an app that instantly compared the Best Buy price to those of other retailers. She found that she could get the same item on the Amazon.com website for only $106.75. Mary bought the Garmin from Amazon right on the spot from her smartphone. By downloading apps, smartphones can take pictures of the barcode on any item and instantly and list price comparisons of local stores and/or online prices.

PRICE FLOORS AND PRICE CEILINGS

Government impedes market correction because government policies can change what the market looks like, but they cannot thwart the market. A minimum wage law may establish a price floor above the equilibrium wage by mandating a minimum wage for all employees. Notice there is no unemployment at the lower wage. When the government mandates a higher wage, suppliers hire fewer workers, while at the same time, more people join the workforce because of the higher wage. The number of workers wanting a job exceeds the number of workers a business wants to hire. In a free market, adjustments would occur; the wage would drop to the point where the quantity demanded equals the amount supplied, restoring full-employment. When the government imposes a minimum wage, we end up with permanent unemployment. Employed persons who make more money benefit from the law, but we now have more people unemployed.

So is a national minimum wage law good or bad for the economy? The answer depends on what the government's mandated wage is in comparison to the equilibrium wage rate. The higher the mandated wage is above the equilibrium wage, the greater the unemployment. You also have to consider that a small business is affected more than big a big one. Creativity and growth stems from small start-up businesses and less so from big companies; thus, a high minimum wage law could adversely impact growth over the long haul.

RENTAL PROPERTY

The government can also mandate price ceilings with rent control. These laws impede market forces and distort the market. Government-imposed low rent results in a shortage of rental property in the area affected by the law. When the quantity demanded is greater than the quantity supplied some people are harmed because of the shortage.

How else could we offer more rental units at lower prices? The government could lower taxes and impose fewer restrictions on property owners. A shift to the right of the supply curve would result in more rental units. So why do we have rent control laws which end up hurting almost everyone? Politics is the answer. Most voters do not understand economics, so they do not vote for politicians who favor landlords.

A RIGGED MARKET

In 2021 amateur investors ganged up on Wall Street heavyweights and beat them at their own game. It all started with the company GameStop. The company hit hard times in 2020 with online competition and the pandemic. Smelling the blood in the water, powerful hedge funds decided to short the company's stock. Shorting a stock is when you borrow shares from a broker, sell them and then replace the shares you borrowed by repurchasing them at (hopefully) a lower price and keeping the difference. In other words, when you short a stock, you position yourself in the market so that you gain from a price decline. But if the stock price increases, you lose.

Reddit is a social news discussion website. Within this community is a group named WallStreetBets with almost six million participants. This group took a contrarian strategy, buying GameStop stock through Robin Hood, a financial trading app. Thanks to their sheer numbers, it pushed up its price, increased demand, causing billions of dollars in losses for the hedge funds who shorted the stock.

But this is a rigged market with control in the hands of major Wall Street firms who can influence demand and supply for their gain. Nasdaq, an American stock exchange market, paused trading in the stock to stem the hedge funds' losses, thus putting downward pressure on demand. Next, the National Securities Clearing Corporation raised the capital requirements for Robinhood, and online platforms banned WallStreetBets, claiming their content was "hateful and discriminatory." Then, Robinhood, astoundingly, shut down the buying of those stocks earmarked by the Reddit investors. Contrary to its name, Robinhood is a platform that favors the rich over the poor.

SUMMARY

A good or service has value depending on its usefulness and level of scarcity; economists define scarcity as there is not enough of something to go around to everyone who wants it at a zero price. Something can be useful, but it may not have much value unless it is also scarce. Something can be very scarce, but it will not have value unless it is also useful. Usefulness and scarcity determine the market value.

Demand and supply curves indicate the usefulness and the level of scarcity of goods and services. They do this by revealing how many units consumers are willing and able to buy at various prices. The supply curve is a graphic representation of the relationship between product price and quantity of product that a seller is willing and able to supply at every possible price. Economists measure price on the vertical axis and quantity supplied on the horizontal axis. The demand curve is a visual representation of how many goods or services consumers will buy at each possible price. It plots the relationship between quantity and price.

The price at which demand equals supply is the point toward which a free market will move. If the price is above this equilibrium price, the units supplied will be greater than units demanded, and the resultant surplus will encourage the supplier to lower price. If the price is below the equilibrium market price, the units demanded will be greater than units supplied, causing a shortage and a higher price.

Demand and supply curves are always changing, causing market prices to change. The swiftness or slowness of these changes depends on the nature of the market. Government policies and other factors can retard the forces of demand and supply. When prices are not free to fluctuate, the change will take place more slowly, and the market will look different, but Mr. Market is still king, we cannot thwart the market indefinitely.

CHAPTER 5
MONEY AND BANKING

Money is an asset that is generally acceptable as a medium of exchange. Individual goods and services, and other physical assets, are priced in terms of money and are exchanged using money as a common denominator rather than one good for another, as in barter, exchanging one good for another. Money enables an economy to produce more because it reduces the time spent by sellers and buyers in arranging transactions. Other important functions of money are its use as a store of value or purchasing power (money can be held over a period of time and used to finance future payments), a standard of deferred payment (money is used as an agreed measure of future receipts and payments in contracts) and as a unit of account (money is used to measure and record the value of goods or services.

Money is useful and scarce. Money can be anything that signifies credits and debits in a financial transaction. Forms of money have different liquidity levels; the more accessible money is to spend, the greater its liquidity. Cash can be very liquid, but you cannot rent a car or pay your mortgage with cash. Checks are liquid when paying your bills through the mail, but it may not be easy to cash a check in other situations. The general price level

CHAPTER 5: MONEY AND BANKING

determines the value of money; deflation increases the value, and inflation decreases the value.

What are the various uses of money? People use money as a unit of account, store of value, a standard for deferred payment, or a medium of exchange. If I say a Cadillac car is worth $40,000 and a Ford is worth $20,000, I am using money as a unit of account. If I put $5,000 in a savings account, I am using money as a store of value. When I pay for something over time, I am using money as a standard of deferred payment. When I buy goods and services, I am using money as a medium of exchange.

MONETARY POLICIES

Monetary policies are policies of the Federal Reserve. During inflationary periods the Fed will tighten the money supply and during periods of unemployment it will loosen the money supply. It is easier to stem inflation than it is to combat unemployment because the Fed cannot force people to borrow money. An unemployed person is not going to borrow money just because interest rates are lower.

John Maynard Keynes mentions the liquidity trap in his book *The General Theory of Employment, Interest, and Money*, 1936. Although monetary policies can effectively stem inflation, they may be ineffective during times of unemployment because money can get trapped in banks. The solution to this liquidity trap is for the government to borrow money from banks and then spend it. Keynes called this process priming the pump.

The Federal Reserve's Regulation D requires depository institutions to keep enough cash reserves available to meet their net transaction accounts' immediate withdrawal requests. The federal reserve requirement determines how much a bank has to keep in reserve. Requiring banks to have a reserve requirement helps prevent bank panics. The current reserve requirement is zero.

The Fed can influence a bank's liquidity by changing open market operations, the discount rate, the federal funds rate, and reserve requirements. According to section 19 (b) of the Federal Reserve Act (Act), transaction account balances maintained at each depository institution is subject to reserve requirement ratios of zero, three, or ten percent. Currently, the reserve requirement is zero. ZIRP, Zero Interest Rate Policy, is a Fed's strategy to push interest rates down to zero. Once a country follows a ZIRP policy, the central bank can no longer lower interest rates, making monetary policy ineffective. Low-interest rates benefit banks who borrow money from the Federal Reserve but hurt savers.

Open Market Operations

Open market operations are the most common monetary policy. Just as the stock market is where people can buy or sell stock shares, the open market is where people buy and sell bonds (securities). Suppose you buy a bond for $8,000, and the face value is $10,000. If the maturity date on the bond is five years from the day you bought it, you can demand payment of $10,000 from whomever you purchased the bond on this maturity date. Now imagine two years after you bought the bond, you decide to sell it. You can sell your bond on the open market for whatever someone is willing to pay (a bond can be bought and sold several times up to the maturity date). The market determines the bond price, whatever the buyer and seller agree. Whoever owns the contract when it matures can receive the face value from the original issuer.

There is an inverse relationship between interest rates and bond prices. When interest rates increase, bond prices fall; and when interest rates decline, bond prices rise. Why is this? If you owned a bond that has not matured yet and you want to sell it when interest rates increase, you have to lower the bond price to attract buyers. However, when interest rates fall, you can sell your bond at a higher price because potential buyers cannot go elsewhere quickly and receive favorable interest return on their savings.

When banks purchase securities from the Fed or in the open market, their excess reserves decline because they have less cash and more securities. When banks sell securities, their excess reserves increase because they have more cash.

Suppose we have an unemployment problem and the Fed decides to increase the money supply to increase demand. The Fed may buy X millions of dollars of bonds from banks or buy bonds in the open market, let's say $100 million worth of bonds. We can postulate that the Fed purchases $50 million of bonds from commercial banks and $50 million from government bond dealers, business corporations, and individuals. When a commercial bank sells $50 million worth of bonds to the Federal Reserve, its bond holdings decline by $50 million, and the Fed credits the bank's reserves by $50 million. The bank's liquidity increases as excess reserves increase. If people borrow more of this money, aggregate demand will increase.

Congress did not establish the Federal Reserve for the sole purpose of making a profit, although it is a virtual money machine.

The Fed's official goal is to improve stability by tempering the twin problems of inflation and unemployment. The most common monetary policy is buying or selling securities, which the Fed can do either from banks directly or at the Open Market. Suppose the Fed goes to the Open Market and purchases $50 million worth of bonds from the General Motors Corporation. As payment for the bonds, GM receives a check for $50 million and makes a bank deposit, increasing its reserves by $50 million.

Now let's say the Fed fears inflation. Instead of buying securities, it will sell securities to commercial banks or the public. Consequently, banks' excess reserves decline as securities are exchanged for cash. The loss of banks' liquidity should lead to a decline in loans and a reduction in aggregate demand, putting downward pressure on prices. How does the Fed encourage banks to buy or sell securities? If the Fed wants to buy securities, it will offer a high price for them. Because the return on a bond is the difference between the purchase price and the face value, a higher price will encourage bondholders to sell bonds now rather than later. On the other hand, if the Fed wants to sell securities, it lowers prices, increasing the spread between the purchase price and the face value.

Discount and Federal Funds Rate

The discount rate is the interest rate that banks pay when they borrow money from the Federal Reserve. Discounting a loan means that the borrower pays interest up-front rather than later. A bank borrows from the Fed when it finds that its reserves have fallen below the required level or if it needs to temporarily build up reserves to fund new loans or demand deposits. The federal funds rate is the interest that banks pay when they borrow money from one another. The only two interest rates that the Fed controls are the discount and federal funds rate.

A higher discount rate makes it more expensive for banks to borrow money from the Fed, and a lower rate makes it less expensive. During periods of inflation, the Fed wants banks to borrow less money, and during periods of unemployment, the Fed wants banks to borrow more. Changing the discount rate affects the financial community because bankers, business people, and investors decide based on the discount rate. Therefore, a change in the discount rate and the federal funds' rates signal how the Fed manages the nation's money supply.

The prime interest rate is the banks' rate on short-term loans made to large commercial customers with the highest credit score. The prime interest rate is the lowest rate banks offer to anyone at any point in time; although the government subsidizes some loans, these loans may be lower than the prime interest rate at times. When the Federal Reserve lowers the discount rate, the prime interest rate generally declines, and, after a time lag, other interest rates fall. The same is true when the Federal Reserve raises the discount rate; the prime interest rate eventually increases. It does not always work like this because banks decide whether to raise or lower their interest rates.

Changing Reserve Requirements

The Federal Reserve will require depository institutions to hold more of their assets in reserve if it wants to reduce the money supply. Prices eventually decline because less money is circulating. Alternatively, the Fed can reduce reserve requirements in a recession. Changing reserve requirements is the least used monetary policy because changes can adversely affect a bank's business plan.

ORGANIZATION

The two decision-making bodies of the Federal Reserve are the Board of Governors and the Federal Open Market Committee (FOMC), with the Board of Governors being the primary decision-making body. The President appoints each of the Board's seven members and submits his nomination for approval to the Senate. Board members serve one 14-year term, exceptions being the chairperson and vice - chairperson who do repeating four-year terms with the President's approval. The seven board members and five Federal Reserve Bank presidents make up the FOMC. The New York bank president serves as a permanent member of the FOMC, while other bank presidents rotate each year. The FOMCs sole purpose is to make decisions regarding the buying and selling of securities.

The Federal Reserve is technically autonomous, not a part of the federal government. In earlier years, the Fed made decisions based on economics and not politics, whereas today, it acts as a partner to the federal government and the world's central banks. The same people own all the central banks. Consequently, long-run economic growth has taken a back seat to short-run stimulus policies.

HISTORY OF THE FEDERAL RESERVE

Will Rogers used to say that the three great inventions since the beginning of time are fire, the wheel, and central banking. Congress chartered the first central bank in the United States from 1791 to 1811. But Congress abolished the bank in 1811, and in 1816 it chartered its successor. President Andrew Jackson rescinded the second bank in 1833 for the following reasons:

- It concentrated the nation's finances.
- It exposed foreign interests.
- It served to make the rich richer.
- It had too much control over Congress.
- It favored northeastern states.

The Federal Reserve got its start on Jekyll Island, then a privately owned island off the coast of Georgia, in 1910. This group represented a financial trust that controlled approximately ¼ of the world's wealth. The Federal Reserve was to break the money trust grip, but they were the money trust! These participants represented the nation's most powerful banks and had financial roots in Europe's largest banks. The American institutions included the J.P. Morgan companies and the banking conglomerate of William Rockefeller, Kuhn, Loeb, Company and the Rothschild banks of England and France and the Warburg banking consortium of Germany and the Netherlands.

The Fed makes most of its money by earning interest on US government and mortgage-backed securities. Presently the Fed owns the vast majority of mortgages in America and 62% of all US government bonds. The Federal Reserve also makes money through interest on banks' loans and selling stock in the Federal Reserve System to member banks. After the Fed meets its annual operating expenses and pays the Consumer Financial Protection Agency ten percent at the end of each fiscal year, it gives the rest to the United States Treasury.

End the Fed is a book by Doctor Ron Paul, a former US Senator, in which he challenges the usefulness of the Federal Reserve. Most people think of the Fed as an indispensable institution without which the country's economy could not properly function. But Dr. Paul draws on American history, economics, and fascinating stories from his own long political life to argue that the Fed is both corrupt and unconstitutional. It is inflating currency today at nearly a Weimar or Zimbabwe level, a practice that threatens to put us into an inflationary depression where $100 bills are worthless.

FDIC

The government established a public agency in 1933 called the Federal Deposit Insurance Corporation (FDIC) because of the frequent bank failures between 1930 and 1933. The FDIC aims to promote stability by instilling customer confidence in banks by insuring each bank account up to $250,000. The FDIC can also serve as Receiver for a bank's assets in the case of bankruptcy. Receivership means that the FDIC pays insurance money to the depositors and assumes the responsibility to sell and collect the failed bank's assets.

COMMERCIAL BANKS

The US banking system consists of a network of privately owned commercial banks chartered by the states or the federal government. Commercial banks can be national or state-chartered. All national banks belong to the Federal Reserve System. About one-half of the total assets reside in the following six banks: Bank of American Corporation, JP Morgan Chase and Co., Citigroup Inc., Wells Fargo and Co., Goldman Sachs Group Inc., and Morgan Stanley.

The federal government protects banks from losses but then regulates them. This relationship has consequences because banks are continually finding ways to thwart the regulations, and in turn, the government penalizes banks for their irregularities or illicit acts. For example, Goldman Sachs Group, Inc. paid $550 million to settle claims by the Securities and Exchange Commission (SEC) that it misled investors in 2010. When Bear Stearns and Washington Mutual, two financial firms, faced bankruptcy in 2008 because of fraudulent activity, the federal government encouraged JP Morgan to acquire their assets. Then, in 2012 the SEC fined JP Morgan Chase & Co. $13 billion for its transgressions but primarily for Bear Stearns and Washington Mutual's sins. Here we have JP Morgan helping out the federal government, and then the government penalizes the bank for the failed firms' transgressions. In the future, American businesses will think twice about doing favors for the federal government.

POLICY CHANGES

There has been a significant change in Fed policies since

the financial collapse of 2007-2008. First, Congress granted the Fed permission to pay interest on a bank's reserves, which is potentially problematic in that it discourages banks from making loans to individuals and businesses. Faced with a choice of making loans to the private sector or collecting risk-free interest from the Federal Reserve, many banks have chosen the risk-free option. Consequently, with more money flowing from banks to the Fed, less money is available to lend to the public, despite lower interest rates.

Another significant development since the financial collapse of 2007-2008 was that the Fed announced that it would grant loans to entities other than commercial banks or the federal government for the first time in history. Since 2008, the Fed has been lending money to favored businesses while refusing loans to others. Instead of letting the market decide who gets loans, the Fed now makes many of these decisions.

DEMAND DEPOSIT MULTIPLIER

The banking system can multiply money from every deposited dollar, depending on the reserve requirement. The following explanation makes two assumptions: that all banks are exactly meeting their reserve requirement and that banks can lend out all of their excess reserves. For the sake of simplicity, let's assume that all reserve requirements are 50 percent, though they differ, and ten percent would be more realistic.

Consider what happens when someone deposits $100 and writes a check against it. The bank will keep $50 in reserve to meet the reserve requirement and lend out $50. Whoever borrows the

$50 will spend or invest it, so let's suppose this person spends it on clothing. The clothing store deposits the $50 in its bank. When the second bank receives the $50, it will keep $25 and lend out $25. Whoever borrows the $25 will spend it, and whoever gets the $25 will put it in their bank. Now the third bank will keep $12.50 and lend out $12.50, and so on to the last penny.

The demand deposit multiplier determines how much total spending increases when someone makes a bank deposit. The formula is $D = 1/R$, where R represents the reserve requirement. In the above example, the required ratio is 50 percent or ½; therefore, $D = 1/$ ½ or 2. Taking the multiplier two and multiplying it times the initial deposit of 100 dollars, total spending increases by 200 dollars.

POLICY DECISIONS

When the multiplier is two, the Fed will increase the money supply by one-half of the desired goal. For example, to increase the money supply by $200 billion, the Fed will initially increase the money supply by $100 billion to achieve this increase.

Economics is not an Exact Science

It would be easy to assume economics is a science by which we make accurate predictions and sound policies, but nothing could be farther from the truth. The truth is that monetary policy can be pro-cyclical rather than counter-cyclical because life is unpredictable. A pro-cyclical policy accentuates the business cycle's swings, and a countercyclical policy is one that tempers the swings of the business cycle. Monetary policy intends to temper the wide swings of the business cycle; in other words, the intent is to promote countercyclical policy rather than pro-cyclical policy, but the opposite is often the case.

CONFLICTING MONETARY POLICIES

Keynesian economists favor discretionary policies, meaning the Fed should make decisions based on the situation. Austrians prefer a rules-based approach, meaning the Fed should base policy on a predetermined set of rules.

Monetary policies can be ineffective because consumers and businesses may choose not to borrow money. Despite lower interest rates, excessive inventory may hinder business people from borrowing more money, and unemployed persons cannot afford to borrow more money. Lower rates may also encourage wealthy individuals, financial institutions, and businesses to lend their funds to foreign borrowers if foreign interest rates are higher than American interest rates.

The most damaging consequence of low-interest rates is the impact on savings and investing. Artificially low interest rates may increase demand in the short run, but economic growth ultimately depends on a country's ability to save and invest. Low-interest rates discourage savings and discourage investment in new plants and equipment because less money is available for investors to borrow. These easy money policies hurt the elderly the most because they often depend on interest income for their livelihood.

QUANTITATIVE EASING

When the Federal Reserve buys securities, it can pay for them with existing funds or with newly created money, which economists call monetizing the debt or quantitative easing. To pay for mortgages and other securities, the Fed has credited banks with electronic deposits—called reserve balances or bank money. The Fed creates this money out of thin air by simply pushing a few keys on its computer. This process of creating new money has exploded since the financial collapse of 2008.

Austrian economists believe that the very existence of quantitative easing as a policy tool creates unpredictability, as traders speculate when and whether the Fed will intervene again. By replacing large decentralized markets with centralized control by a few government officials, the Fed distorts incentives and disrupts free market business practices.

Austrians believe the Fed is ineffective at stimulating the economy because much of this new money fails to circulate in the general economy. There are three reasons for this:

- Banks invest money in the derivatives market, a worldwide market where investors can speculate on future events.
- The New York Federal Reserve Bank has concluded that money creation increases the racial wealth gap due to the Cantillon Effect. Modern Monetary Theory (easy money policies) favors investors over wage earners because the monied class always

has first dips in the loanable funds market, and wage earners get the dregs. This is the Cantillon Effect.

■ The federal government gets a large share of this new money because it is the Fed's largest borrower; the Fed monetizes the national debt.

The Fed's expansionary monetary policy can hurt foreign nations. When the United States increases the money supply, dollars on the global market tend to increase, reducing the dollar's value and raising the value of other currencies. For example, when Brazil's currency, the cruzeiro, increases in value relative to the dollar, Brazilian products become more expensive to non-Brazilians, thus hurting the Brazilian economy.

NATIONAL CLEARINGHOUSE

Have you ever wondered what happens to your check after you cash it? Before we find out, let's see what happened to checks "in the days of old." In the early days of banking, each bank in a town would give all the checks it had received to a messenger, and the messenger would walk to each bank and exchange the checks for money. One day, a tired and thirsty messenger stopped at a pub. While he was waiting for his pint, another messenger came in, tired and thirsty from his daily walk. They sat together, each with his bag of checks, discussing their routes. After talking a bit, they discovered they could save themselves some legwork by exchanging their respective checks.

Consider messenger A on his way to Messenger B's bank with $750 worth of checks. Messenger B is on his way to Messenger A's bank with $800 of checks. They realized they could meet halfway and exchange checks and write the word "cancel" on them, which proved that they had exchanged checks dollar for dollar. In other words, if you owe somebody $700, and that person owes you $700, would you give one another 700 dollars? But what about the extra $50 that Messenger A owes Messenger B? In this case, each messenger (each bank) keeps track of who owes who what. It was not long before these meetings became the first clearinghouse. The Federal Reserve serves as a common clearinghouse for American banks.

FEDERAL RESERVE and GOVERNMENT

The Fed keeps currency in good condition by replacing worn bills with new coins from United States Mints and new paper from the Bureau of Engraving and Printing. This replacement of paper money is needed because the life span of dollar bills, especially one-dollar bills, is extremely short. The Fed also acts as a bank for the federal government, allowing it to write checks against its deposits with the Fed.

Monetizing the Federal Debt

The partnership between the Fed and the federal government increased after the financial collapse of 2008 when the Fed engaged started monetizing corporate debt. In recent years the Federal Reserve has bolstered the economy by purchasing Treasury bonds.

An Austrian economist would say the Fed's policies affect the economy adversely by weakening the dollar and reducing purchasing power. These policies also increase the risk of future inflation, conceal the unsustainable fiscal policy's actual cost, transfer wealth from savers to debtors, and reduce long-term economic growth.

A Keynesian economist would favor these policies because they stimulate demand. The Fed defends QE because low-interest rates will continue to make mortgages affordable and help the housing industry recover. The Fed also believes that purchasing large portions of the US national debt helps keep the federal government solvent.

Fed and the Dodd-Frank Act

The Federal Reserve is responsible for implementing provisions of the Dodd-Frank Wall Street Reform and Consumer Protection Act (the "Dodd-Frank Act" or "DFA") in conjunction with other government agencies. The Consumer Financial Protection Bureau (CFPB), an independent entity housed within the Federal Reserve, has the legal responsibility of protecting consumers by promoting transparency and consumer choice and preventing abusive and deceptive practices in consumer financial products and services.

The legislation also strengthens systemically important financial institutions, gives the government an important additional tool to wind down failing financial firms and establishes an interagency council to detect and deter emerging threats to the financial system.

Austrian economists criticize the agency because, in part, they believe that the American taxpayer is on the hook for such bailouts and that this practice is becoming epidemic. Institutions that the Federal Reserve declares as systemically important now have an implied taxpayer safety net. But the government cannot define what "systemically important" means.

Austrian economists point out that low-interest rates are beneficial for borrowers but not for retired people dependent on interest as a significant income source. Low-interest rates may also affect the dollar's value because foreigners will take their money out of dollar-denominated assets and buy assets from other countries. Another criticism of the Consumer Financial Protection Bureau is that it promotes big government by politicizing financial decisions and undermining the free market's critical aspects.

GLASS-STEAGALL / THE VOLCKER RULE

Banks, who used depositors' money to make risky investments, aggravated the Depression of the 1930s. Many of these investments soured as the Depression progressed. Consequently, in 1933 Congress passed the Glass-Steagall Act, calling for the separation of commercial and investment banking. Commercial banks used depositors' money to make loans, whereas investment banks used funds from wealthy individuals to invest in risky ventures. The government did not regulate investment banks, giving them licenses to take sizeable risks. This suited wealthy people because risky investments are more fun and potentially more profitable than safe investments. The government did regulate banks so that they could not put depositors' money at substantial risk.

Investment banks made enormous profits in activities that the Glass-Steagall Act made unlawful for commercial banks, and commercial banks wanted to share in the bounty. The lobbying efforts of the investment community succeeded in convincing Congress to repeal the Glass-Steagall Act with the Financial Services Modernization Act of 1999. The Financial Services Modernization Act allowed banks to compete with investment banks in these risky ventures, leading to a repeat of the banking collapse of the 1930s in 2007. Since then, Congress passed the Volcker Rule, which is a watered-down version of the Glass-Steagall Act.

Congress passed, and President Obama signed into law the Dodd-Frank Wall Street Reform and Consumer Protection Act in 2012. Part of that law, the Volcker Rule, prohibits proprietary trading by banking entities—in effect, reintroducing a significant portion of the Glass-Steagall Act's static divide between banks and security firms.

Proprietary trading occurs when a firm trades stocks, bonds, currencies, commodities, derivatives, or other financial instruments with the firm's own money instead of customers' money. The Volcker Rule is 77 pages long with another 882 pages of explanation. The Commodity Futures Trading Commission had only five days to adopt the rule to meet a political and arbitrary deadline. Regulators are given discretion to craft ever more complicated and convoluted regulations and offer a booming business for lawyers to interpret the law.

An example of proprietary trading is banks using their financial capital to make bets in the derivatives market. The Volcker Rule does not affect US Treasuries and financial instruments issued by Fannie Mae and Freddie Mac. Therefore, the Volcker Rule allows Wall Street giants to make enormous bets on the direction of US government bonds and debt issued by government-sponsored enterprises, such as Fannie Mae and Freddie Mac. Like many recent financial regulations, the Volcker Rule offers banks and investors powerful incentives to lend the government money rather than lending to private businesses, thus reducing liquidity in America's capital markets.

Austrian economists point out that the Dodd-Frank Law encourages rent-seeking because businesses can sway regulators and gain favorable treatment. In the fog of uncertainty, business interests will always trump noble intentions. When transgressions do occur, regulators are usually the last ones to detect them. The Volcker rule is complex because Dodd-Frank requires regulators to identify proprietary trading, which is almost impossible.

If you understand the basics behind the Glass-Steagall Act of 1933 and the Dodd-Frank Wall Street Reform and Consumer Protection Act of 2012, you get a glimpse of differing philosophies. The Glass-Steagall Act was simple and required little government involvement. Once Congress made the distinction between commercial banks (firms that receive depositors' money) and investment banks (banks that accept money from wealthy individuals and institutions for the sole purpose of investing), the government took a hands-off approach toward investment banks. In contrast, the Volcker Rule is an attempt to micromanage what banks can and cannot do. Because there is no longer a distinction between commercial banks and investment banks, the Volcker Rule tries to replicate the Glass-Steagall Act's protections.

TROUBLED ASSET RELIEF PROGRAM

The repeal of the Glass-Steagall Act in 1999 encouraged banks to take excessive risks, which paved the way to the financial collapse of 2007-2008. On September 18, 2008, former Treasury Secretary Henry Paulson and Fed Chairman Ben Bernanke held a meeting with legislators to propose a $700 billion bailout for banks. Paulson reportedly told Congress, *If you do not do this, we may not have an economy on Monday*! The Emergency Economic Stabilization Act, which implemented the Troubled Asset Relief Program (TARP), became law on October 3, 2008. Most of the money went to financial institutions.

The Emergency Economic Stabilization Act of 2008 codifies into law the concepts of "rent-seeking" and "moral hazard." As you may recall, rent-seeking occurs when special interest groups buy favors from Congress, and moral hazard occurs when the government takes on the losses of failing businesses. Rent-seeking and moral hazard is a dangerous combination because it benefits the few at the expense of the many; it tends to privatize profits while socializing losses.

After leaving TARP a couple of years later, Barofsky wrote about his Washington DC experiences. In the book, he reveals how he was stymied every step of the way, especially by the Treasury Department. The government shuffled more than 700 billion dollars out the door with almost no oversight.

CHAPTER 5: MONEY AND BANKING

SUMMARY

Congress passed the Federal Reserve Act in 1913, thus creating a central bank for the United States. A central bank deals mainly with other banks and the government and assumes broad responsibilities in the national economy's interest, apart from earning profits. Each Federal Reserve bank has at least one reserve branch bank that carries out the Federal Reserve's policies.

The United States banking system is composed of Federal Reserve banks and commercial banks that may or may not be members of the Federal Reserve System. The federal government charters all national banks, and all national banks are obligated to follow the Fed's rules and regulations. For example, member banks have to buy stock in the Federal Reserve System and obey the Fed's reserve requirements. States charter state banks, and they have the option of belonging to the Federal Reserve System or not. Banks must maintain liquidity to retain the confidence of their depositors. Maintaining this liquidity is perhaps the most potent constraint in making a profit.

The Federal Reserve helps the federal government by serving as its bank, offering checking services, aiding the Treasury in borrowing money, and keeping currency and coins in good condition. The Fed also acts as a national clearinghouse for checks.

The Federal Reserve has the responsibility of regulating the nation's money supply. If we have an inflation problem, the Fed will make it more challenging to borrow money. If people borrow and spend less money, the decline in demand will eventually decrease prices. On the other hand, if unemployment is a problem, the Fed will make it easier to borrow money. Monetary policies are the collective actions of the Federal Reserve.

The Board of Governors is the decision-making body of the Federal Reserve System. The Board is composed of seven persons appointed by the President of the United States and confirmed by the US Senate. These seven persons and the presidents of five Federal Reserve Banks make up the Federal Reserve System's open market committee. The New York bank president serves as a permanent member of the committee; the other banks rotate as members annually. The Federal Open Market Committee has authority regarding open market policies, which is the buying and selling of government securities (bonds). The Fed is technically autonomous, but members of the Board of Governors are political appointees, so there is usually a working relationship between the Federal Reserve and the federal government.

The Federal Reserve's three tools are buying and selling government securities, raising or lowering the discount rate, and raising or lowering reserve requirements. The most common is buying and selling government securities, and the least used policy is the raising and lowering of reserve requirements. Changing reserve requirements can cause instability in the banking system.

Monetary policies are generally more effective against inflation than unemployment. By restricting the money supply, demand eventually has to decline, leading to a decline in prices. It is a different story when we have an unemployment problem. The Federal Reserve can make it easier for people to borrow money, but it cannot force them to do so.

Despite our efforts, monetary policy is guesswork. It is also sobering when you realize that policymakers make decisions based on their worldview, which may or may not be how the world works. Thinking that monetary decisions always have their roots in economics is naive. The Fed has evolved from being an independent central bank to be a central planner in partnership with the federal government.

CHAPTER 6
GOVERNMENT

A lthough Keynesians favor a strong central government and Austrians disfavor it, they do agree that we need government to provide the following:

- uniform weights and measures.
- the rule of law.
- public goods.
- protects against social costs.
- encourages merit goods.
- provides a strong national defense.
- helps the poor and disadvantaged.

PRIVATE AND PUBLIC GOODS

Goods that you would purchase at the store, like food and iPads, are examples of private goods. Individuals consume private goods, and these persons need not share with someone else. Multiple people can share a public good; one person's use does not exclude others. Once the military has its defense in place, everyone can benefit from the protection (not rival), and it would be too costly to exclude anyone from the benefits (not excludable).

Public goods, such as schools, national defense, and roads benefit all members of society. Public goods have a free-rider problem. The fact that a public good is not rival and not excludable makes it challenging to produce privately. This free-rider problem prevents the private market from supplying public goods. Therefore, the government must provide society with public goods.

MERIT GOODS

A merit good is a good that benefits everyone. Public education is a merit good as well as a public good. The government discourages some things, like cigarettes, and declares others illegal, for example, heroin. ObamaCare charges higher premiums on smokers. Most European countries mandate labeling of GMOs, Genetically Modified Foods, and companies must state ingredients. Merit goods can be encouraged by first-party and third-party laws. For example, the law requiring motorcycle drivers to wear helmets protects the driver (the first party) but does not cover other people (the third party). In contrast, laws that mandate automobile inspections protect first and third parties.

SOCIAL COSTS

Social costs are costs that the system forces unto society, such as pollution, unsafe working conditions, and nonrenewable natural resources depletion. Without government intervention, businesses will pay less, and society will pay more. Society has to pay for a water processing plant when faced with polluted water, and when companies do not invest in safe machines, the worker is vulnerable to accidents.

The more we put into national defense, the fewer resources we have for everything else. The more we put into alternative goods, the less we have for national security, etcetera. Rational choice says that Society should pursue additional government activities if the expected marginal benefits exceed the expected marginal costs. It all gets back to the economic problem.

Free Markets Have Social Costs

Consider the socially conscious Alpha Paper Company. Alpha safely disposes of its waste products, installs safety devices, and recycles its byproducts. Beta Company does not have a social conscience, does not install safety devices, does not recycle, and pollutes. Because Beta Company passes as many costs as possible onto society, its costs are lower than Alpha company's expenses. Consequently, because Alpha Company must charge a higher price than Beta company, most consumers go with the lower price.

Minimizing Social Costs

Society must limit social costs. Should states or the federal government pay the most? Texas has sued the federal government, challenging the federal government's ability to take over the state's air pollution authority. Texas claims the federal government is impeding its legal rights and has asserted that the EPA's actions violate the Clean Air Act. Presently the federal government requires power plants to obtain greenhouse-gas permits from the federal government (instead of the state) before building new facilities or making significant modifications to existing ones. There is a trade-off between a clean environment and growth, but the solutions are not obvious.

Conflicting Opinions

American farmers have diverted 40 percent of corn production from food to fuel. Yet, the National Academy of Sciences claims that ethanol production increases greenhouse gas emissions and raises food prices worldwide. The National Association of Clean Air Agencies claims that burning higher ethanol blends results in increased nitrogen oxides and other harmful pollutants.

So why is the EPA supporting ethanol? One reason is that the ethanol industry has significant political influence. Think, "rent-seeking." Another reason is that we have a government agency with the authority to make decisions based on one person's beliefs; the EPA administrator can issue mandates without Senate approval.

Yes, we need laws that protect the environment, but what happens when authorities support unreasonable anti-growth policies that cause unemployment? When the economy fails to grow sufficiently, our infrastructure denigrates.

LENGTHY & DETAILED LAWS

Let's suppose Congress passes a law against ties. We can easily enforce the law because everyone knows ties. Now suppose Congress passes a law forbidding anyone to wear a beautiful tie. Who is to say what is beautiful? Now we need a government authority to determine what is beautiful and what is not attractive. The door is thus left open to arbitrary decisions, politics, and rent-seeking. The 2,700 pages Affordable Care Act (with 22,000 pages of regulations) and the 2,300-page financial reform bill are examples of "the beautiful tie" situation. Both bills are so lengthy and complicated and contain so many ambiguities that no one understands the whole of it.

FREE MARKET IS JEOPARDIZED

Events have jeopardized the free market in favor of the top one-percent of income earners. When the government partners with the Federal Reserve and orchestrates low-interest rates, who are the beneficiaries and who are the losers? The wealthy benefit the most because they are the closest to the money; they receive the lion's share while average savers receive less interest. This Cantillon Effect transfers money from the have-nots to the haves.

RULE OF LAW

The auto bailouts in 2008 turned contract law on its head when the White House subordinated bondholders' rights to those of its union allies, contrary to bankruptcy laws. The government imprisons people for killing bald eagles, yet companies that produce wind power are exempt from the law. Congress passed ObamaCare, yet declared the law null and void for members of Congress and their staff. The Environmental Protection Agency issued new ethanol mandates on 143 refineries. Still, it exempted one lucky refinery that happens to be under the patronage of a key Senator who was up for re-election.

CHAPTER 6: GOVERNMENT

The executive branch has made thirty-eight changes to the Affordable Care Act without Congressional involvement. According to the Constitution, the Executive branch of government has the responsibility to execute the laws that Congress makes faithfully, but it does not have the authority to make laws.

In George Orwell's novel, *1984*, authorities monitor Oceania's citizens and issue fabricated news stories that adhere to the party line. Authorities convince citizens to worship a mythical government leader called Big Brother, while it gives nonsense statements like "WAR IS PEACE, SLAVERY IS FREEDOM, IGNORANCE IS STRENGTH." In this Orwellian world, power is centralized, and the establishment punishes anyone who speaks or acts against the official narrative.

In his book *Animal Farm*, George Orwell shows how power corrupts, no matter how noble the intent. In the book, an animal group centralizes control over the farm to ensure equality. The novel ends with the barnyard commandments, high on their righteousness, reducing the commandments to only one, which is *all animals are equal, but some are more equal than others.*

Millionaires, health care providers, pharmaceutical companies with Coronavirus vaccines, energy companies, subprime dealers, favored groups, and bird killers are more equal than others. Section 230 of the US Communications Act provides immunity for website entities, such as Facebook, YouTube, Twitter, etc., from third party content. The government gifts these favored entities with the best of two worlds. They have the protections of a neutral platform, such as a newspaper that reports on the news. Still, they have the privileges of publishers, who can be opinionated while accepting only like minded viewpoints. These platforms have become more powerful than governments and are the new rulers of the universe. So long as the system picks the winners and losers, there will always be some groups more equal than others.

GOVERNMENT PROGRAMS

The idea of redistributing wealth stems from the Progressive Movement in the last quarter of the 19th century. Americans had tamed the frontier, built cities, grew businesses and expanded worldwide. But not all citizens shared in the new wealth. The Progressive Movement addressed these deficiencies.

Social Security (SS)

The payroll tax, called FICA, funds the Social Security Program. Monthly benefits depend on past earnings and the age at which the retiree receives benefits. Instead of letting the funds accumulate in the SS Trust Fund and earn interest, Congress has used the money for general purposes and replaced it with non-negotiable IOUs. A non-negotiable IOU is a bond that persons cannot sell on the secondary market.

Because social security is a pay-as-you-go system, it is the world's largest Ponzi scheme. A Ponzi scheme is one in which the participants receive returns on their contributions from the latest contributors. Suppose that I assure you and others that I am an excellent investor and I can triple your money in five years. But, instead of investing your money in the markets, I pay you returns from the money I collect from new entrants. The scheme begins to fall apart when there is a lack of new people.

Unemployment Benefits

Unemployment benefits compensate people who have lost their jobs and demonstrate that they are actively seeking employment. The program does not include persons entering the workforce for the first time, nor does it cover persons who have quit their jobs. Congress decides how long unemployment benefits will continue, but states administer the program. A state can borrow money from the US Treasury if it runs out of funds but must pay the money back.

Medicare

By 2030, only 2.4 workers will support one older person. Medicare is a federal social insurance program providing health insurance coverage to sixty-five and older people. It also ensures some permanently disabled people who are younger than sixty-five. Medicare has four parts:

- Part A is Hospital Insurance.
- Part B is Medical Insurance.
- Part D covers prescription drugs.
- Medicare Advantage plans, also known as Medicare Part C, provide an alternative means for beneficiaries to receive Parts A, B, and D benefits.

With more than 1.5 million baby boomers a year signing up for Medicare, the program's future is one of the most critical economic issues for seniors. Health care costs are the most unpredictable part of retirement, and Medicare remains an excellent deal for retirees, who can reap benefits worth far more than the payroll taxes they paid in during their careers.

Medicaid

Medicare and Medicaid are government sponsored programs designed to help fund healthcare costs. Congress established both programs in 1965. Congress designed Medicare to help with long-term care for the elderly while Medicaid covers healthcare costs for the poor.

There is a critical difference between Medicare and Medicaid, whereas Medicare is an insurance program, Medicaid is akin to an equity loan. With Medicaid, the state may have the right to everything upon the recipient's death, up to the cost of Medicaid benefits received. For example, if a person had received $50,000 in benefits, upon that person's death, the government will confiscate his assets up to $50,000. There are some limits to what the state can seize, as in the case of hardship or to protect a surviving spouse, but the law is exceptionally complex and leaves a great deal to the government's discretion.

James Madison warned in the Federalist Papers about laws *so voluminous that we cannot read them, or so incoherent that we cannot understand them*. Medicare and Medicaid are examples of such laws. A typical provision of Medicare reads like this:

In the case of a plan for which there are average per capita monthly savings described in section 1395w–24 (b)(3)(C) or 1395w–24 (b)(4)(C) of this title, as the case may be, the amount specified in this subparagraph is the amount of the monthly rebate computed under section 1395w–24 (b)(1)(C)(i) of this title for that plan and year (as reduced by the amount of any credit provided under section 1395w–24 (b)(1)(C)(iv) [2] of this title.

Supplemental Security Income (SSI)

Supplemental Security Income (SSI) is a federal program funded by general tax revenues and establishes a uniform, national minimum income for people unable to work. The program helps the elderly, blind, and disabled people who have little or no income and provides funds to meet food, clothing, and shelter needs.

Patient Protection & Affordable Care Act

The name "Affordable Care Act" or "Obamacare" is usually used to refer to the law's final, amended version. The law expands the Medicaid program to cover more people with low incomes. However, Medicaid expansion was put on hold for several states when the Supreme Court ruled that it would be optional and up to each state whether to expand these programs or not.

Health and Human Services Department

As part of the Affordable Care Act, the government transformed the Health and Human Services Department into a massive venture capital investor for health care. Awash in ObamaCare dollars, HHS has a growing investment portfolio that includes everything from new insurance companies to health-care start-ups to information technology. HHS already makes more grants than all other agencies combined, and it is the patron of health care for about one of three Americans via Medicare, Medicaid, or both.

The problem is that HHS misspends its resources. Ernst & Young's, a large accounting firm, did an annual external audit of the HHS balance sheet and found that HHS cannot accurately track its spending. The agency violates numerous federal accounting rules explicitly written for the bureaucracy to say nothing of public companies' financial reporting. The HHS inspector general has revealed that his team could barely monitor HHS because its staff is too busy chasing the criminals exploiting HHS's incompetence.

Housing and Urban Development

The United States Department of Housing and Urban Development (HUD) is a federal Cabinet. It became a Cabinet department in 1965, as part of the "Great Society" program of President Lyndon Johnson. HUD is the lead Federal agency responsible for programs concerned with the nation's housing needs, fair housing opportunities, and communities' development.

Federal Housing Administration

The Federal Housing Administration (FHA) does not make loans but provides mortgage insurance on loans made by FHA-approved lenders. Because the FHA protects lenders from losses, lenders can reduce their standards. The FHA exhausted its capital reserves in November 2012 and asked for additional funding from the US Treasury, something it had not done in its 78-year history. Together with Fannie Mae and Freddie Mac, federal agencies now back nine in ten new mortgages.

UNFUNDED LIABILITIES

If the government confiscated the total adjusted gross income of American taxpayers, plus all corporate taxable income, it would not be nearly enough to balance the budget. David M Walker, a former US comptroller general, says that the country's "dysfunctional democracy" is preventing a return to "fiscal sanity." He believes that there is a difference between the short-term deficit and the structural deficit problem. We have a long-term structural deficit problem because of unfunded liabilities. The only way to solve America's economic problems is to phase in structural changes over time.

TAXES

The government foresaw a collection problem in 1942 when it doubled income taxes. In those days, taxpayers sent a check to the government once a year, but as spring arrived in 1943, it became clear that many citizens might not file tax returns. Henry Morgenthau, the Treasury secretary, confronted colleagues about the nightmarish possibility of mass tax evasion by saying: *Suppose we have to go out and arrest five million people!*

Now meet Beardsley Ruml, a man of ideas who observed that people preferred installment payments. Instead of citizens paying their annual taxes all at once, the government could make businesses collect taxes from each paycheck and forward the funds directly to Washington. No longer would the employee ever have to face his tax bill square in the eye.

Our current income tax system has exemptions and deductions. You and your spouse and each of your children count as an exemption. Each exemption is worth X amount of dollars.

Deductions are the second category, such as the interest paid on your mortgage and charitable donations. If these two categories (exemptions and deductions) are more than the government-stipulated standard deduction for that year, you fill out the long-form and itemize your deductions.

A flat tax is a tax that levies the same percentage on all income levels with few exemptions and deductions. A national sales tax, or a flat tax, would be efficient, easy to implement, and promote efficiency gains.

Lengthy and Complicated Tax Laws

Our present system allows politicians to make concessions and exceptions for favored groups, giving big corporations an advantage over their competitors. A popular gambit for Congress is to make the tax laws so lengthy and convoluted that only the big players will have the resources to comply with the regulations.

Compliance costs are making American companies less competitive around the world.

Consider the Federal Work Opportunity tax credit, which typically lowers a company's taxes by thousands of dollars per employee. However, the credit frequently goes unclaimed, primarily because it is such a hassle to win approval. It requires extensive paperwork for each worker, which can take a year or more to process. While many companies say it is too complicated to claim tax breaks, the ones who try can find themselves embroiled in complex disputes with the Internal Revenue Service.

Tax Incidence

The federal government relies primarily on the personal income tax, which is a progressive tax. The graduated income tax (sometimes called a progressive income tax) system taxes citizens based on their ability to pay, meaning the wealthy pay more proportionately than low-income people. State governments rely on income and sales taxes, and local governments rely on property taxes.

The "benefits received" principle taxes persons the most who receive the most benefits from the tax. One example of this principle is a tax on gasoline where each gallon of gas; therefore, the people who drive the most pay the most.

A tax on food is regressive. Jack has an annual income of $100,000, and Bill has a yearly income of $50,000. Both Jack and Bill have similar eating habits, and both spend about $200 weekly on groceries. Bill bears the more significant burden because a dollar to him is worth more than a dollar to Jack.

NATIONAL BUDGET

The federal budget year begins September 1 of each year. In the previous January, Congress receives a budget proposal from the Executive Branch regarding spending for the next fiscal year. After the House makes adjustments, it passes the budget to the Senate. After modifications, the Senate passes it on to the President, who sends a modified version to the House. Around and around she goes until September 1, when the new fiscal year begins. However, it rarely works out this way; instead, a continuing resolution temporarily extends spending at the previous year's level.

It isn't easy to access spending from one year to the next because of off-budget expenditures. Off budget spending is spending that Congress does not count as part of the official budget. Off budget spending, in short, is a tool used to conceal the actual cost of government programs. Features of Social Security and the US Postal Service are off-budget. In Social Security, the trust funds are off-budget, and administrative expenses are on a budget. Any losses that the Federal Reserve may incur, Congress considers off-budget spending. Any money appropriated to Fannie Mae and Freddie Mac, Congress considers off-budget. President Ronald Reagan liked to quip that only in government is failure rewarded with more money. Here is an example of "Washington Speak." If Congress spends $100 in year one and says that it plans to spend 200 dollars in year two, but instead spends $150 in year two, it claims it cut spending by $50!

THE US, CHINA and RUSSIA

The 2010 Wall Street Reform and Consumer Protection Act, known as the Dodd-Frank Law, marked a government policy change. This Law encourages market concentration by forming a partnership between the government and big business. Businesses that the government does not favor are at a disadvantage because they do not have the same support that the government gives to big business.

We live in a neo-liberal world where there are few restraints on big business. Instead of the government regulating big industry, big business and government are partners in crime where Congress passes laws and doles out money to the favored class. We no longer have a free enterprise system, an impartial system with no monopolies. Unrestricted freedom has allowed monopolies, oligopolies, and cartels to flourish.

The best example of this partnership is the military-industrial complex. Companies like Raytheon and Boeing hire an army of lobbyists who convince Congress to engage in this and that war. About one-fourth of the total budget goes to the military who supports over 800 military installations worldwide. The US has been active militarily in Somalia for over thirty–years and Afghanistan for more than fifteen–years.

This top-heavy spending on the military puts the US at a disadvantage with China and Russia. While the US spends money on things that quickly deteriorate and become obsolete, China, with only one military base, and Russia, with four outside their borders, have more capital to invest in their economies. China and Russia are playing the long game; they act like a chess player who sees moves far into the future, while the US is more like a checkers player who only sees the next move.

While the US is experiencing a concentration of power, China does not tolerate unfair competition. When Chinese regulators accused Alibaba of violating its anti-monopoly law, Authorities fined Alibaba 2.8 billion dollars. The country's tech giants, particularly the ones operating in the financial sector, have been under scrutiny from the Chinese government amid its increasing power.

In recent years, the US's money supply has increased 25 percent more than nominal GDP, a 25 percent increase in liquidity. When the money supply increases more than goods and services grow, the result is always inflation and always benefits the wealthy class over the poor. China's expansion in the money supply has kept pace with its increase in GDP. So, China and Russia have borrowed nothing from the future, whereas the US has stolen from its future growth.

IDENTIFYING THE PROBLEMS

Austrian economists believe that long and detailed bills, like the 2,700-page health care bill and a 2,300-page financial reform bill, cause problems. A bill can include any volume of unrelated topics and can be of any length. Even Nancy Pelosi, the former majority leader in the House of Representatives, stated that she did not know all that was in the health care bill—but that we would like it after it became law. Is this any way to run a country? Some states have given their governors line-item veto power, whereby the governor can go through a bill line by line and veto portions of it. However, when President Bill Clinton used the line-item veto, the Supreme Court declared it unconstitutional.

Pork barrel spending is a constant obstacle to growth. Pork barrel spending appropriates government spending for localized projects secured primarily to bring money to a representative's district, regardless of its contribution to the nation's growth and prosperity.

Austrian economists question regulators' policies as they try to micromanage complex markets and engage in favoritism. Austrians believe a better strategy would be to simplify the rules to avoid unintended consequences while taking politics out of markets.

The federal income tax's century-long history teaches us that higher tax rates give Congress a reason to invent more loopholes. These carve-outs are always politically motivated; favored industries and businesses will get the tax breaks - whereas less favored companies will pay the full tax increase.

SUMMARY

Public goods benefit everyone, despite who pays for them. For example, government-subsidized education benefits everyone by encouraging society members to be law-abiding and productive citizens. A robust national defense benefits everyone. Our road system would not be possible without a strong government. The government taxes gasoline and uses the money to build and repair roads. Without government, we would have a road system based on tolls, which would be grossly inefficient.

We also need the government to protect us against social costs. Social costs are costs of production for which businesses bear no responsibility but pass the costs onto society. Examples of social costs are:

- pollution
- unsafe working conditions
- nonrenewable resource depletion.

In a free market, there is a tendency toward high social costs. The government's challenge is to intervene without sacrificing productivity, growth, and personal liberty. Government promotes merit goods and helps disadvantaged people. Merit goods and services that the government considers desirable, the government encourages by subsidies or regulations. In this aspect, the government is acting as a parent-guardian over us. Public education and healthy foods are examples of merit goods. Sometimes the government will discourage or forbid the sale of unhealthy or dangerous goods, such as drugs and cigarettes.

A free enterprise system is efficient in producing goods and services and promotes growth and prosperity. Unrestricted freedom, however, can lead to monopolies. Big business can exploit the consumer by charging high prices, producing less quantity, and offering inferior quality goods.

CHAPTER 7
FISCAL POLICY

A ustrians believe that enduring surpluses are impossible because Say's Law assumes that "supply creates its own demand." When businesses pay wages, the market wage will be sufficient to clear the market. There may be a mismatch between demand and supply, but prices, wages, and interest rates adjust toward full-employment. Thus, a free-market system will tend toward full–employment where leakages equal injections. Leakage is money leaving the system, and an injection is a money entering the system. Government spending is an injection—taxes is a leakage. Exports cause injections—imports cause leakages.

AUSTRIANS & THE GREAT DEPRESSION

Laissez-faire, the idea that government intervention is unnecessary during periods of unemployment, was popular before the Depression of the 1930s. For example, in 1921, the economy recovered quickly from Depression without government intervention. President Warren Harding and the Federal Reserve paused as to what to do, but before they could do something, the Depression was over.

Between 1930, when Herbert Hoover was President, and 1932 when the country elected Franklin Roosevelt (FDR), history books disagree about events. Most educators believe that President Hoover's laissez-faire policies aggravated the decline and that Roosevelt saved American capitalism with his New Deal Programs. Austrians, however, believe that the New Deal prevented adjustments that would have helped the economy recover. The book *Meltdown* by Thomas Woods Jr., 2009, is a compelling read on the subject.

President Herbert Hoover favored active fiscal policies by launching public works projects, raising taxes, and extending emergency loans to failing firms. He lent money to states for relief programs and encouraged businesses to increase worker's wages. In the presidential election of 1932, Roosevelt chided the Hoover Administration for too much spending and intervention. However, when FDR took office in 1933, he expanded programs by raising taxes, establishing public works and social welfare programs, and encourage investments by keeping prices as high as possible. Austrians believe that these Hoover-Roosevelt policies prevented the economy from seeking its full-employment equilibrium.

KEYNES and THE GREAT DEPRESSION

In his book, *The General Theory of Employment, Interest, and Money*, 1936, the British economist John Maynard Keynes argued that the neoclassical viewpoint was valid only under specific circumstances and not in the general sense. Thus, he included the word 'general' in the title of his book. Although Roosevelt and Keynes encouraged big government, a relationship never developed because Roosevelt was not an economist, but he knew he had to do something.

Keynes believed the economy could tend toward less than full–employment. Austrians believe a free–market, the economy will always grow to full-employment. Keynes believed that the government should sell securities, increase spending, and lower taxes to increase demand so to shift the economy from a less than full employment equilibrium to a full-employment equilibrium.

How does a demand increase influence prices and production? The answer is 'that all depends on the slope of the aggregate supply curve' If the aggregate supply curve is more horizontal than vertical, an increase in demand will affect output more than prices.

THE EMPLOYMENT ACT OF 1946

Although government spending decreased after 1945, the post-World War II era witnessed government expansion. The Employment Act of 1946 gave the federal government the responsibility of using all reasonable means to promote maximum employment, production, and purchasing power. The Employment Act of 1946 opened with this declaration:

> *The Congress hereby declares that it is the continuing policy and responsibility of the Federal Government to use all practicable means consistent with its needs and obligations and other essential considerations of national policy, with the assistance and cooperation of industry,*

agriculture, labor, and state and local governments, to coordinate and utilize all its plans, functions and resources.

THE WORLD'S STANDARD CURRENCY

The fact that the American dollar is the world's reserve currency has masked its economic problems. Despite missteps and enormous debt, the dollar has remained strong on the international market. This singular privilege keeps the demand for the dollar high despite America's prolific policies. However, several countries are co-opting the dollar by using alternative currencies to settle international transactions.

FISCAL POLICIES

Fiscal policies are only effective when people perceive them to be permanent. Consumers tend to make decisions based on their perceived permanent income, not on temporary changes. For example, assume you expect a raise next year, but you want to buy a computer today. So you say to yourself, *Self, let's buy the computer because I can afford it with my pay raise.* However, when the federal government makes a quick policy change, like mailing everyone $1,500, the effect is negligible because consumers' expectations do not change.

Fiscal Policies and Deficit Spending

Increases in federal spending and federal deficits have threatened the economic system. So why does Congress borrow money every year? The reasons are a bloated defense budget, generous social programs, and interest on a growing national debt. Another justification for deficit spending is what Keynesian economists call the balanced budget multiplier. The theory goes like this. If consumers have a dollar, they will save part of it and spend the rest; when the government has the dollar, it consumes all of it.

Deficit spending helps prevent a liquidity trap. People earn income, deposit the money in a bank, the bank lends it out, people deposit the money in another bank, and so forth. Economists call this process the circular flow of money. In this fashion, banks act like your heart. Your heart pumps blood to different parts of your body, distributing oxygen and nutrients. When this circulation slows, you become anemic. When banks cannot lend out enough money, they will lower interest rates. However, what happens if these lower interest rates are inadequate? What happens if consumers and investors do not borrow enough money despite the lower interest rates? Then the economy stagnates. The only solution is for the government to borrow these sterile savings and inject the money into the economy. Economists call this action priming the pump.

Fiscal Policies and Stagflation

When inflation and unemployment coexist, economists say we have stagflation. Stagflation presents us with a policy dilemma because when the government restricts the economy, unemployment worsens; when the government stimulates the economy, inflation worsens.

So, can we fight both problems concurrently? The answer depends on whether we consider the short-run or the long-run. In the short run, we have few options. In the early 1980s, the solution to stagflation was to curb inflation and allow unemployment to worsen. Once we broke the back of inflation by restricting the money supply, policymakers turned their attention to the unemployment problem.

In the long run, we have more promising options. Despite what we do in the short-run, we must boost efficiency gains and growth. By establishing stable monetary policies, reasonable taxes, and regulations, the aggregate supply curve will shift to the right, resulting in lower prices, increased output, and more jobs.

Fiscal Policies and Rent Seeking

Fiscal policies affect small business and non-union workers the most and big business and union members the least. Big business and unions win concessions from Congress while they stick everyone else with the tab.

Fiscal Policies and Unions

There is a difference between private and public unions. Over the past several years, there has been a decline in private unions, unions that bargain with businesses, but an increase in public unions. Private unions have less bargaining power than do public unions. Companies have to make a profit, but governments can increase taxes.

If unions bargain for wage increases exceeding their productivity gains, costs increase. These higher costs can have a significant or negligible impact on the company. If an industry faces an inelastic demand curve, it can raise the price to make up for the higher costs and still make a profit. If the business faces an elastic demand curve, revenue will decline with a price increase. What does elasticity have to do with private and public unions? The bargaining power of private unions is limited because most businesses face an elastic demand curve. If they meet union demands, their costs increase. If they raise the price to make up for this increase, they may face insolvency.

Public unions have more bargaining power because governments provide goods and services with few substitutes; therefore, they face relatively inelastic demand curves. Governments also have more control over their prices; they can raise taxes, and citizens have no choice but to pay. Because public unions have more bargaining power than private workers, they can successfully pressure governments for higher wages and benefits.

Austrians and Fiscal Policies

Austrians point out that when special interests vote themselves more benefits than society can afford, they diminish efficiency. What happens when leaders are more concerned with wealth distribution and less concerned with growth? Draw a line and label it security floor. This line represents a financial floor by which the government will not allow most people to fall below, like what ObamaCare does when it guarantees everyone minimum health care. Now draw another line above this and label it success ceiling. Where does the money come from to maintain this security floor? It has to come from people who have the money. So, the higher the security floor, the lower the success ceiling.

A second reason Austrians disfavor discretionary fiscal policies is that the natural rate of unemployment can be tricky to determine. If economists estimate that the normal rate of unemployment is 4 percent, but it is 5 percent, at 4 percent, we may find ourselves trying to fix something that is not broken, thus making things worse.

A third reason Austrians disfavor fiscal policies are time lags. Three lag effects restrain all government programs. First, the government has to identify the problem; second, politicians need to make decisions; third, authorities need to implement the plan. By the time these three lag effects take place, the problem may not exist. Policy actions, although well-intentioned, tend to be destabilizing rather than stabilizing.

Austrians believe discretionary fiscal policies would work better if we had a wise king who had absolute power. When something went wrong, this king would know what to do and act quickly. But we have an independent president who may or may not have the support of Congress, 535 Congressmen, and two political parties.

Fiscal Policies & the Keynesian Multiplier

There is a multiplier effect on each dollar injected into the income stream. Let's assume that people will spend one-half and save one-half of each dollar they earn. Economists define savings as money earned but not spent. Savings can be taxes, social security, insurance, and similar payments.

CHAPTER 7: FISCAL POLICY

When people earn income, the marginal propensity to consume (MPC) measures how much consumers tend to spend out of that income. The marginal propensity to save (MPS) estimates how much people tend to keep out of that income. Therefore, if people spend and save one-half of their income, then the MPC is ½, and the MPS is ½.

Now let's assume that Sandra receives $100. She will spend $50 buying a widget from Susan. Now that Susan has received $50, she will spend $25 to buy a widget from Bill, who spends $12.50 to buy a widget from Sam, who in turn, spends $6.25, and so forth. Out of the original $100 injection, total spending increased by about $200, that is, $100 + $50 + $25 + $12.50 + $6.25, etc. Instead of going through this mathematical process, we can use the Keynesian multiplier, which is 1/MPS. If MPS is ½, the multiplier is two.

Now suppose economists calculate that national income has to increase by $2 billion to achieve a full-employment equilibrium without causing inflation. If the government were to spend an additional $2 billion, national income would increase by $4 billion, causing inflation. Instead, the government should increase spending by one billion. If discretionary fiscal policies are to be effective, we must understand the value of the multiplier.

Austrians have reservations concerning discretionary fiscal policies and the Keynesian multiplier because it is challenging to expect policymakers to have the facts and expertise to do the right thing. Furthermore, since when did Congress make decisions based on economics? Even assuming that politicians knew anything about economics, a big assumption, they will almost always make political decisions.

Another problem with discretionary fiscal policies is the nature of government spending. Policymakers have traditionally made decisions without considering the flow. When Congress decides to raise taxes by five percent, it assumes that government revenues will increase by five percent. But life is always a flow situation. If the government raises taxes, this will have some effect on taxpayers' behavior, depending on who is bearing the tax burden. The increase in taxes will hurt spending, saving, and investing, which will eventually impact economic growth and government revenues.

Fiscal Policies and the Accelerator

The accelerator measures secondary spending. That is, sometimes there is a multiplier beyond the simple multiplier because of induced investments. For example, suppose the government spends one-billion dollars on a new highway. If the MPS is ½, we know that a one-billion-dollar increase will generate two-billion dollars of spending. There is also an accelerator effect because the new highway will induce businesses to invest in gas stations, restaurants, and motels.

Suppose businesses invest $1.5 billion to take advantage of the new highway. Because the MPS is still ½, there are multiple effects of two on this $1.5 billion. In other words, the $1.5 billion in increased investments would eventually cause $3 billion of additional spending. Instead of the initial one-billion leading to an increase of two billion expenditure, it is five billion dollars, two billion because of the multiplier, and three billion because of the accelerator. The accelerator effect complicates decisions for policymakers. The accelerator effect is more likely to take place when the economy is operating at full-capacity and less likely to take effect when there is less than full employment.

Austrians Debunk Keynesian Economics

Austrian economists believe that it is not possible to guide the economy to a full-employment equilibrium because:

- First, we have to know if we are in a full-employment equilibrium or not. If not, we have to know where to relocate the economy.
- Next, we have to know the multiplier and the accelerator's value.
- Congress has to agree on policy.
- We have to consider the national debt.
- Then we have to know where we are on the Laffer Curve.

After knowing all of this, Austrians would question whether constructive policies are possible given our budget and debt restraints and the foreign sector's dynamic effect. According to Austrian economic thought, the success of Keynesian policies would only be possible in the minds of academics who have no idea of how the real world works. Do you think that the President and members of Congress know or care about this stuff?

Fiscal Policies and the Laffer Curve

What effect will an increase in taxes have on government revenue? The answer is that all depends. Starting from a low tax rate, an increase in taxes will increase government revenues because citizens will see the benefits. However, when taxes increase beyond a certain point, government revenues will decrease because the high taxes will discourage citizens from working, save, and invest. The higher taxes will also encourage more people to escape to other countries or give incentives to participate in the underground economy.

AUTOMATIC STABILIZERS

Austrian and Keynesian economists disagree on discretionary fiscal policies but agree on automatic stabilizers. For example, the unemployed automatically receive benefits if they qualify. Automatic stabilizers limit strong upswings of the business cycle and help stimulate the economy during recessions.

Austrians favor monetary policies, the free market, and automatic stabilizers. They believe that the demand management idea of the Keynesians is a fairy tale. Keynesians believe that if we measure economic activity (inflation, unemployment, GDP growth, balance payments, etc.) and use our monetary and fiscal policies correctly, we can guide the economy to a full-employment equilibrium.

SUMMARY

According to popular beliefs, during the 1800s and early 1900s, if we had a problem with unemployment, the economy would make adjustments, and we would move back toward full-employment. Therefore, the federal government should practice laissez-faire—it should let the market make the necessary adjustments.

The government took a laissez-faire approach to the 1920s depression and an active approach to the 1930s Depression. President Warren Harding paused in 1920, and by the time he decided to take action, the Depression was over. In contrast, the Great Depression of the 1930s and John Maynard Keynes's theories changed popular opinion toward demand management economics.

Congress passed the Employment Act of 1946, which gave the federal government the responsibility to use all practical means to promote maximum employment, production, and purchasing power. Government spending as a percentage of the total spending has increased a lot since the 1930s.

Discretionary fiscal policies that are counter-cyclical are the exception and not the norm. For example, the multiplier and the accelerator effect make it challenging to know policy outcomes. Most economists agree that automatic stabilizers are helpful, but there is disagreement on discretionary fiscal policies. Austrians support monetary policies, the free market, and automatic stabilizers. Keynesians support discretionary fiscal policies.

CHAPTER 8
INFLATION

Inflation is a pervasive rise in the average price level. People expect low inflation rates, but high rates can destroy economies, especially when it is erratic and unanticipated. Inflation is always a monetary phenomenon; it is always caused by the monetary authorities increasing the money supply more than goods and services.

Under a gold standard, we were protected from inflation because authorities could not increase the money supply unless its gold holdings increased at the same time. We have not been on an actual gold standard since before the 1920s, but up until 1971, nations could exchange dollars for gold upon demand at the US Treasury. The final nail into the gold standard's coffin came to an end when President Richard Nixon closed the gold window in 1971 and refused convertibility. At this point, we opened the door to inflation because the new system eliminated the ties between the dollar and gold. Nixon's closing the gold window gave inflationary factors a free hand to wreak havoc on the economy.

FARMING

Ancient Rome had financial problems between 218 A.D. and 268 A.D. because of huge military expenses, generous public works programs, growing uneven distribution of wealth, deteriorating infrastructure, and high taxes. Rome's economic problems led to the wealthy purchasing more and more of the farmland, thus relegating most of the population to serf status. The same thing is happening today. At the top of the list is Bill Gates, who now owns most of the nation's farmland, about thirty percent, over 240,000 acres. John Malone is the largest landowner with 2.2 million acres or 3,500 square miles of land, and Ted Turner owns two million acres. The top eight landowners own more than a million acres each. Jeff Bezos, the founder of Amazon, owns more land than Bill Gates, but not as much farmland.

Whoever controls the farmland controls the food, and whoever controls the food controls the population. Henry Kissinger has said, *Control oil and you control nations, control food and you control people.* Historically this phenomenon of land ownership has typically come at the end of empires when they are ready to collapse.

CURRENCY DEBASEMENT

Rome's problems began when it debased the currency. Debasement is primarily associated with coins made from precious metals, such as gold and silver. Debasing a currency means authorities make coins with a mix of precious metals and base metals instead of purely precious metals, thus the term debasement.

The more the government adds base metals to a coin, the more a currency is debased.

When debasement led to inflation, Emperor Diocletian blamed merchants for the inflation, and in 301 A.D., he attempted to fix prices by edict. He tried to nullify the market, the demand, and the supply of money, by wage and price controls. His decree led to shortages and hoarding, which led to penalties against hoarding. These policies made all citizens wards of the state and crashed the economy.

Modern-day debasement occurs when monetary authorities, the Federal Reserve, increase the money supply more than goods and services increase. Because gold or silver does not back up the dollar, it is a fiat currency. When a fiat currency increases, each unit's price or value declines; thus, it takes more of them to buy things.

BRETTON WOODS MONETARY SYSTEM

World War II had a devastating effect on the global monetary system. A plan for restoring order came in 1944 at Bretton Woods, New Hampshire when 730 delegates from 44 Allied nations met to replace the British currency as the standard for settling international transactions. Because the United States held substantial gold reserves, countries saw the US dollar as the best replacement of the weakened British pound. Thus the Bretton Woods system was born. The new system linked the dollar to gold at a pre-determined rate of $35 per ounce, and the system linked all other currencies to the dollar.

CHAPTER 8: INFLATION

By pegging currencies to gold at fixed rates, all nations knew the relative worth of currencies. This Bretton Woods system elevated the US dollar as demand shifted from the British pound to the US dollar. Because the US agreed to exchange dollars for gold at a fixed rate of $35 per ounce, the system had confidence in the dollar. If a nation lost faith in the dollar, it could convert its dollars to gold.

America's inflation problem began in 1969 with a President facing re-election. President Richard Nixon inherited a recession from Lyndon Johnson, who had simultaneously spent generously on the Great Society and the Vietnam War. Congress, despite some protests, continued to fund the war and continued to increase social welfare spending. America's inflation averaged five-to-ten percent per year in the 1970s.

President Nixon imposed wage-price controls in 1971, ran budget deficits, and announced he was a Keynesian. However, the deficits caused foreigners to flee the dollar in return for other currencies. Nixon told a national television audience that the gold standard, or what little of it remained, was kaput. The United States declined to value the dollar at 1/35th of an ounce of gold and thus made the dollar a fiat currency. Fiat money is a government-issued currency that is not backed by a physical commodity, such as gold or silver, but rather by the government that issued it.

Nixon was able to enhance his political career by convincing the Fed to increase the money just as voters were casting ballots. Consequently, in 1973, inflation was 9% and reached a high of 14% by 1980. The reason that the Bretton Woods system of fixed exchange rates faltered is the fact that countries were experiencing widely different inflation rates.

If the US has an inflation rate of ten percent per annum, the dollar's value declines by ten percent. Suppose England is having an inflation rate of seventeen percent, the British pound declines by seventeen percent. If Germany has an inflation rate of four percent, the German mark will decline by four percent. So how can countries trade with one another with fixed exchange rates? They can't. The only reason that the Bretton Woods system worked after 1944 was that all countries experienced similar inflation rates. Therefore, the values of their currencies relative to one another did not change much. Even under the Bretton Woods System, countries were allowed to alter their currencies to gold up to a certain point. But the widely different inflation rates of the late 1960s overwhelmed the system.

PETRODOLLAR SYSTEM

Despite pressure from foreign nations to protect the dollar's value by reining in excessive government spending, Washington displayed little fiscal constraint. It continued to live far beyond its means in the 1960s. It had become evident to all that American lacked the essential fiscal discipline that could prevent the destruction of its currency. Americans figured out how to 'game' the system for its benefit, leaving foreign nations in an economically vulnerable position. Washington knew that the 'dollars for gold' had become entirely unsustainable. But instead of seeking solutions to the global economic imbalances that America's excessive deficits had created, Washington's primary concern was how to gain an even greater stranglehold on the economy.

After America had tasted the sweet fruit of excessive living at the expense of other nations, there was no turning back. But to maintain global dollar demand, the Washington elites needed a plan. America found the solution in Saudi Arabia. The Nixon Administration held a series of high-level talks with Saudi Arabia and other oil-producing nations, intending to require the dollar as a standard currency in oil sales. In exchange, Washington offered military assistance and protection for the region's oil fields. After Saudi Arabia agreed to accept only dollars in exchange for its oil, other oil-producing nations followed suit. In essence, instead of dollars for gold as under the Bretton Woods arrangement, the new system became dollars for oil arrangement. This arrangement is called the Petrodollar System.

CREDIT CREATION vs GROWTH

Severing the ties between money and gold obliterated any constraints on cash and credit, and a new economic paradigm took shape; economic growth took a back seat to credit creation and consumption. There is a grave danger that this credit-fueled economic paradigm will break down. In the book, *The New Depression*, Richard Duncan explains that we no longer have capitalism; instead, we have creditism. Creditism has created extraordinarily rapid growth for decades, but it has hit its limit because we can no longer pay off national debts without money creation.

When the United States stopped backing dollars with gold in 1971, the nature of money changed. The new paradigm removed all constraints on money and credit creation. Economic growth ceased to be driven by capital accumulation and investment as it had been since before the Industrial Revolution. Instead, credit creation and consumption began to move the economic dynamic.

FIAT CURRENCIES

Fiat currencies have made inflation problems a certainty. Under the gold standard, we could not increase the money supply unless we increased the quantity of gold, but there is no limit to expanding the money supply with a fiat system. In his book *Leverage – How Cheap Money Will Destroy the World*, Karl Denninger shows how money creation could destroy economies worldwide. He presents an inside look at how moneyed and powerful interests debase the dollar through the willful and intentional failure to honestly represent short and long-term mathematical truths that underlie all economic systems. He shows how, if imbalances are not corrected, financial crises will reoccur again and again.

THE PRICE MECHANISM

Prices must be allowed to fluctuate because prices play three roles: they convey information, give incentives, and provide finances. If the supplier sets too high a price, the surplus will force the market price down, and if he sets too low a price, the quantity demanded will be greater than the amount supplied, and the market will drive prices higher. The higher prices will give suppliers an incentive to increase supply because of an increase in profits; the higher prices will also provide the supplier more money to put into new plants and equipment.

CRYPTOCURRENCIES

Some economists prefer to use the term currency rather than money because a fiat currency has value only because the government says it has value, and people believe it. It helps that dollars are legal tender, allowing citizens to pay debts with this fiat currency. On a dollar bill, it states, *this note is legal tender for all debts public and private.* The level of usefulness and scarcity determine the exact value of dollars; if dollars were as plentiful as fallen leaves, each dollar would have little value.

We are on the threshold of a world-wide economic renaissance and the emergence of cryptocurrencies. Cryptocurrency is a digital currency where the system verifies and records all transactions within a decentralized peer-to-peer system using cryptography. The most popular cryptocurrencies are Bitcoin (BTC), Ethereum (Ether), Ripple (XRP), Bitcoin Cash (BCH), and EOS. There are more than 100,000 websites that accept cryptocurrencies as payment. Even Visa is considering adding cryptocurrencies to its payment network.

There is nothing more powerful than an idea whose time has come. The time for peer to peer transactions has come. Is it time for you to enter into this new age? You can enter the world of cryptocurrencies by going to http://bitcoin.com and downloading a wallet. I suggest you start with Bitcoin Cash because the fees are less than Bitcoin. Bitcoin is a currency created in 2009 by an unknown person using the alias Satoshi Nakamoto. The system makes all transactions with no middlemen, that is, no banks or governments. There are no transaction fees and no need to give your real name when you use bitcoins.

How do bitcoins come into existence? People "mine" bitcoins using computers to solve complex math puzzles. Miners are rewarded in bitcoin. According to Cambridge Bitcoin Electricity Consumption Index, bitcoin's annual carbon footprint is equivalent to Argentina's carbon footprint and the electricity expended is greater than what Ireland consumes. Currently, a winner is rewarded with 25 bitcoins roughly every ten minutes. Bitcoins are stored in a "digital wallet," which exists either in the cloud or on a user's computer. The wallet is a virtual bank account that allows users to send or receive bitcoins, pay for goods, or save money. Cryptocurrencies may be a hedge against inflation.

INFLATION is DECEIVING

Inflation sneaks up on us like a thief in the night. If you get 5 percent interest annually on your savings, but prices increase 7 percent during the year, you lose 2 percent in real terms. Inflation can sneak up on consumers. Suppose you buy a familiar candy bar for what you think is the regular price, but when you get home, you realize that it has only 8 ounces of chocolate instead of 10. A 5 percent increase in a food item and a 3 percent increase in gasoline prices may not seem like much, but small increases can be deceiving over a long period.

INFLATION DISTORTS INFORMATION

Inflation distorts, confuses, and complicates the decision process. Likewise, inflation confuses the producer because price changes do not necessarily show consumer preferences. Uncertainty replaces certainty; indecision replaces decisiveness, and confusion proliferates.

CAUSES OF INFLATION

Demand-pull and cost-push are two types of inflation. Demand-pull inflation occurs when the demand curve shifts to the right relative to the supply curve, causing an increase in the average price level. Cost-push inflation occurs when wages and other costs increase more than productivity increases, thus shifting the left supply curve. Cost-push inflation is more problematic than demand-pull inflation. If prices are high because of high demand, prices will promptly respond to a decrease in demand. However, when prices are high because of high costs, the adjustment process will be slower.

The quantity theory of money ultimately determines the price level. The quantity theory of money is $MV = PQ$, where M is the money supply, V is the velocity of money (how quickly money changes hands), P is the general price level, and Q stands for the number of goods and services or GDP. Thus $P = MV/Q$ showing that prices will increase as the money supply and the velocity of money increases and the number of goods and services decreases.

POSSIBLE REMEDIES

Some remedies for inflation get to the source, while others address only the symptoms. Some remedies are simple while others are more difficult, but all remedies are painful. Possible inflation treatments include reducing the money supply, escalator clauses in contracts, fiscal restraint, a wage-price freeze, elimination of trade restrictions, and productivity gains.

Reduction in the Money Supply

Restricting the money supply would be the best solution to inflation—but this is not as simple as it sounds. Consider what happened in the 1970s. When inflation is persistent, a decline in the money supply will eventually eliminate the problem but only with unpleasant side effects. The reduction in the money supply will cause a drop in consumer demand and business investments, causing an increase in unemployment. As unemployment worsens, there can be a potent political desire to stimulate the economy. Employment improves when the Fed reverses itself and increases the money supply, but this will cause more inflation and the need to restrict the money supply once again. This scenario repeats itself, and each go-around leads to more inflation and more unemployment.

How did we get off this merry-go-round in the 1970s? In 1980, Paul Volcker, then Chairman of the Federal Reserve, decided to keep a tight rein on the money supply. Mr. Volcker became unpopular as we experienced a severe recession in 1980 and 1981. However, he did not give in to the temptation of increasing the money supply to combat unemployment, and the price level eventually subsided. Once he got a handle on the inflation problem, he concentrated on the unemployment problem, and the rest of the 1980s experienced prosperity and moderate prices.

Escalator Clauses

An escalator clause permits changes to a contract, such as basing a worker's wage on the rate of inflation plus a certain percentage. Escalator clauses allow wages to decline as inflation declines without affecting real income. Loan contracts can include escalator clauses by which financial institutions adjust interest rates every year based on the inflation rate. Instead of paying a fixed percentage, the borrower would agree to pay a small percentage, say 2 percent plus the rate of inflation. This way, as the rate of inflation declines, so will loan payments. Meanwhile, the lending institution will make the same real profit on the loan.

Fiscal Restraint

The government can help solve an inflation problem when it decreases spending and increases taxes. Of course, if we increase taxes, we assume that the government will use the money for debt reduction and not spend it, which is a big assumption. Another problem is the impact on special interest groups. Special interest groups are always eager to protect their share of the federal budget, and politicians are reluctant to harm their constituency. The government tries to make an increase in taxes politically acceptable in two ways. First, it will claim the tax increase applies only to the super-rich, and second, it changes the name. Instead of calling it a tax increase, the government will call it a policy that will enhance revenue.

A Wage-Price Freeze

A wage-price freeze always finds someone at a disadvantage, and some business was just ready to raise prices because of an increase in cost, some workers were on the fringe of receiving pay raises. Eventually, we have to lift the freeze to prevent bankruptcies and human suffering. When we remove the freeze, producers will raise prices. A wage-price freeze may be ineffective at bringing down prices of goods most responsible for inflation. During an inflationary period, some goods and services increase in price more than others. For example, Washington cannot control the interest rate on loans without creating all kinds of other problems.

Price controls undermine economic freedom and, in the process, personal freedom. They distort resource allocation by preventing the price mechanism from equalizing supply and demand while enlarging the bureaucracy. Excessive government regulations promote illegal activity by otherwise law-abiding citizens via the underground movement, which deals in cash and pays no taxes. Wage-and-price control programs address the symptoms of inflation rather than the causes and have never been successful.

Increase Productivity

The general price level would decrease if productivity increased enough. The lower costs and lower prices would increase real income and encourage growth. If the government gave businesses more support, such as tax incentives, the positive effects could be significant.

DEFLATION

For centuries until World War II, countries experienced periods of deflation interspersed with periods of inflation. Germany's hyperinflation of the 1920s was followed in the 1930s with deflation that caused widespread economic hardship. Experience shows us that growth is almost impossible when deflation sets in, as consumers and companies cut back spending, believing that prices will fall further, causing aggregate demand to collapse. Wages and prices traditionally hold up, but slumping corporate profits eventually force companies to reduce production and wages, hold off investing, and lay off workers setting off a self-reinforcing downward economic spiral.

SUMMARY

Economists define inflation as a pervasive and general rise in the average price level. People on fixed incomes are hurt the most. Unanticipated inflation can be the most harmful. By correctly anticipating the inflation rate, employers and employees can agree on contracts compatible with the expected inflation rate, but unanticipated inflation breeds uncertainty. When inflation is unexpected, completing contract agreements are more complex, and whoever underestimates the inflation rate will suffer the most. Inflation causes havoc by distorting price signals. It diminishes real incomes and causes unemployment. Inflation can also affect individual freedom as it enlarges the public sector.

There are two types of inflation, demand-pull and cost-push. Demand-pull inflation occurs when an increase in aggregate demand pulls prices up. Cost-push inflation occurs when costs increase, forcing businesses to raise prices. Cost-push inflation is more difficult to remedy because of time lags. If prices are high because of high costs, demand must decline a lot and for a long time before prices fall.

Possible remedies for inflation include:
- a reduction in the monetary growth rate.
- fiscal restraint.
- a mandatory wage-price freeze.
- elimination of trade restrictions.
- an increase in productivity.

Deflation is a persistent and general decline in the price level. Although a reduction in the price level benefits consumers, deflation can be harmful to the economy.

CHAPTER 9
STAGFLATION

E conomists like to say that a recession is when your neighbor is out of work and a depression is when you are out of work! All economists agree that depression is worse than a recession. America has witnessed three significant depressions: 1837, 1893, and the 1930s. Other years of high unemployment occurred in 1857, 1873, and 1907. We had a severe downturn in 1920, but the economy quickly recovered.

A recession is a macroeconomic term that refers to a significant decline in general economic activity in a designated region. It had been typically recognized as two consecutive quarters of economic decline, as reflected by GDP in conjunction with monthly indicators such as a rise in unemployment. However, the National Bureau of Economic Research (NBER), which officially declares recessions, says the two consecutive quarters of decline in real GDP are not how it is defined anymore. The NBER defines a recession as a significant decline in economic activity spread across the economy, lasting more than a few months, normally visible in real GDP, real income, employment, industrial production, and wholesale-retail sales.

The labor force is the number of employed people plus the unemployed who are looking for work. The labor pool does not include the jobless who aren't looking for a job. For example, stay-at-home moms, retirees, and students are not part of the labor force. The Bureau of Labor Statistics measures the unemployment rate by dividing the number of unemployed persons by the labor force. The Bureau surveys about 60,000 households each month, primarily by knocking on doors. Surveyors make their door-to-door trek, asking such questions as the length of job search, age, and status in the household, race, and gender.

The biggest problems in detecting employment are:

- Young people postponing looking for jobs.
- Students who are extending college.
- long-term disability benefits.
- Part-time workers.
- Under-employment.

During World War II, from about 1941 to 1945, there was a substantial influx of females into the labor force. When the soldiers came home, there was a tendency for women to quit their jobs to be full-time wives and mothers. This trend lasted until the 1970s, when an increase in unemployment and prices drove a record number of females back into the workforce. About one-half of the labor force is female, and almost 60 percent of college students are female.

The Bureau of Labor Statistics reports monthly on six categories of unemployment. Persons marginally attached to the labor force are currently neither working nor looking for work but indicate that they want and are available for a job and have looked for work sometime in the past 12 months. Discouraged workers are workers who have stopped looking for work because they found no suitable employment options.

TYPES OF UNEMPLOYMENT

The different types of unemployment are frictional, structural, seasonal, and cyclical. Some are temporary, while others are more deeply rooted.

Frictional unemployment

Frictional unemployment is the temporary unemployment of resources (as labor) resulting from job changes, imbalance of production factors, or short-term lack of mobility preventing continuous employment.

Structural unemployment

Structural unemployment tends to develop around significant changes in an economy, such as moving from an industrial to a technological economy. Displaced workers often remain unemployed. Technology eliminates some jobs and births others. Blockbuster faced bankruptcy because the owners considered themselves to be a video rental business. But their business was not rentals; it was entertainment. Another example is Microsoft. Microsoft thought that Apple Computer would never succeed with its new and novel device, the iPad. However, Apple sold six million units on the first day of sales and has revolutionized the mobile device industry. These events bring about change that alters the economy.

American corporations are at a tax disadvantage compared to the rest of the world. Unlike other countries, profits earned abroad face double taxation, once to the host country and again when the money returns home to America. Consequently, to compete with foreign companies, US corporations have developed tax strategies to keep cash in foreign countries instead of bringing the money home. So instead of using their own money to invest, corporations typically borrow to make investments.

Congress passed the Foreign Account Tax Compliance Act (FATCA) in 2010. FATCA requires all financial institutions to make available to the US internal revenue service (IRS) complete documentation of all their customers who can be considered American citizens. The IRS will then make sure that these people are compliant with American tax laws or face penalties. New rules can change the economy structurally, impacting growth and employment.

Seasonal unemployment

Shifts in the labor force, a change in demand and labor supply, can cause seasonal unemployment. Lifeguards lose their job at the end of summer, migrant workers lose their jobs at the end of the harvest, and carpenters find few jobs in the cold months, and so forth.

Cyclical unemployment

Cyclical unemployment occurs with the ups and downs of

the business cycle, increasing during recessions and decreasing during expansions. Some jobs are more susceptible than others to the vicissitudes of the business cycle. For example, the housing market is one of the first affected at the onset of a recession, and carpenters are often the first to experience the pains of growing unemployment.

Covered and Un-Covered Employment

Covered employment is when an employee qualifies for benefits. Uncovered employees do not qualify for benefits, such as unemployment insurance or social security.

Full-Employment

The concept of full employment has been defined differently by different economists. Keynes defined full employment as the absence of involuntary unemployment. Excessive inventory is what causes unemployment. For example, if a company produces and sells a thousand units a month regularly, it can manage a steady inventory. Now let's suppose that the demand for its product declines, and its warehouse starts to overflow with excessive inventory causing it to reduce production and resources, including labor. If the business continues to have excess inventory, it will reduce prices. Companies that have a heavy debt burden will reduce their prices earlier than debt-free companies. To find the current unemployment rate go to http://www.bls.gov/

Is the unemployment rate an accurate statistic? No, the unemployment rate is not very accurate. Is the unemployment rate a useful statistic to policymakers? Yes. So what is the point? The point is that statistics do not have to be entirely accurate to be helpful. Statistics can be useful when they tell us where we are going and how quickly we are going there. If economists calculate the unemployment rate the same way month after month, year after year, they can at least get an idea of whether things are getting better or worse.

THE GREAT DEPRESSION OF THE 1930s

What caused the unemployment rate to reach 25% in the 1930s? It all started with greed. Many business owners believed that high prices and low wages would guarantee extravagant profits. This scheme worked for a time because of rapid growth that all the inventions and innovations made possible—this was the Roaring Twenties! Eventually, however, the lack of consumer purchasing power led to excessive inventory and growing unemployment. The risky investments that were popular in the 1920s accelerated the downward spiral as investors scrambled to protect their fortunes. The economy quickly headed south without unemployment benefits to prop up consumer demand.

The farming situation compounded the problem because farmers were such a large segment of the population. During World War I, farmers produced record crops and livestock to handle the increase in demand as the war disrupted food harvests in Europe. But in the early 1930s, prices dropped so low that many farmers went bankrupt and lost their farms, thus putting downward pressure on the economy.

The 1930 Smoot Hawley Tariff, increased taxes, and a decrease in the money supply pushed a weakened economy into depression. The Smoot Hawley Tariff diminished demand by raising the prices of foreign products. A 1932 tax increase by the Hoover Administration reduced consumer demand, and when the newly elected Roosevelt Administration increased taxes again, consumer demand took a nosedive. Adding to this downward spiral, the Federal Reserve decreased the money supply pushing consumer demand down even more.

Smoot-Hawley Tariff

The Smoot-Hawley Tariff raised US tariffs to historically high levels. The original intention behind the legislation was to protect farmers against imports. During the 1928 election campaign, Republican presidential candidate Herbert Hoover pledged to support the beleaguered farmer by, among other things, raising tariff levels on agricultural products. But once the process started, it proved impossible to stop. Calls for increased protection flooded in from special interest groups, and soon a bill meant to provide relief for farmers became a way to raise tariffs in all sectors of the economy. When the dust had settled, Congress had agreed to tariff levels that exceeded the already high rates established by the 1922 Fordney-McCumber Act, which was among the most protectionist tariffs in US history.

This high protective tariff made matters worse for several reasons. Higher import prices led to a general price increase putting downward pressure on consumer demand. Because we were buying less from foreigners, they ended up buying less from us. World trade declined 66% between 1929 and 1934.

Fed Decreases the Money Supply

After witnessing the growing unemployment in the early '30s, foreigners started taking their money out of the United States. To counteract this predicament, the Federal Reserve increased interest rates, encouraging foreigners to keep their money in the US. But the increase in interest rates diminished consumer demand.

STAGFLATION

The stagflation of the 1970s proved that we could have both an increase in inflation and an increase in unemployment at the same time, contrary to the Phillips Curve, which showed that we could not have inflation and growing unemployment simultaneously. The reason for this stagflation was a shift to the left of the aggregate supply curve. Supply curves shift to the left with an increase in costs. Businesses cannot afford to produce as much at higher costs than they could with lower costs. There are two reasons why the aggregate supply curve shifted to the left. The first reason is a wage-price spiral whereby powerful unions bargained for pay raises greater than their productivity increase, raising costs. The second reason is that the Organization of Petroleum Exporting Countries (OPEC) raised oil prices. Because oil is essential to almost everything, this caused an increase in costs, thereby shifting the supply curve.

Stagflation led to authorities pulling in opposite directions. Given the option, politicians will want to stimulate the economy; producing jobs and establishing new programs have always been more popular than restrictions. However, the Federal Reserve will choose the opposite course of action for two reasons. First, since Federal Reserve Board members do not have to worry about winning elections, they can concentrate on long-run stability, even if that means more unemployment in the short run. Second, monetary policies are most effective at fighting inflation.

Federal government policies and Federal Reserve policies can cancel one another out, with fiscal policies pulling in one direction and monetary policies pulling in the opposite direction. The federal government will always choose to fight unemployment, and the Fed will tackle the inflation problem. The upshot is that we cannot solve a cost problem with demand remedies. We must solve supply problems with supply remedies.

WHAT TO DO?

Stagflation poses a dilemma for policymakers. All economists agree that we must revitalize the industrial base. If investments were to increase, we could solve the twin problems of inflation and unemployment. The problem is a chicken and the egg situation. Do we focus on raising capital investments and productivity first? Or is it necessary to use monetary and fiscal policies first to stabilize the economy? Austrians favor stable policies concentrating on long-term growth while Keynesians favor proactive policies to remedy short-run problems. Keynes talked about using fiscal policies to fine-tune the economy, meaning we should always guide the economy.

Case for Stable Policies

Economists who favor stable policies, the Austrians, tend to ignore short-run fluctuations. For example, the Federal Reserve should increase the money supply each year to compensate for growth. Suppose the money supply increases at the same rate as the economy grows. In that case, there should be no tendency for inflation, and the federal government should strive for a balanced budget over the long-run, running up deficits in bad times and surpluses in good times.

Case against Stable Policies

Keynesians dislike policy rules because they believe rules become obsolete as circumstances change. When this happens, we need to change the rules to fit the new circumstances. Second, there is a problem in defining money. Third, they tend to be inflexible in an atmosphere of changing conditions.

Suppose the current administration is in favor of fixed rules and follows stable policies. Then unemployment worsens, and the political pressure to do something intensifies. When politicians finally do something, the tendency is to overreact, causing inflation. Alternatively, what happens if the current leadership favors rules, but voters put them out of office? The next administration is not in favor of regulations. Consequently, we could have wide swings from one administration to the next. Whether economists favor active policies or rules, they agree we should pay more attention to lag effects, avoid sharp policy changes, and pay more attention to long-term effects.

Let's Face Reality

So far, we have been discussing strategy as if policymakers (Congress and the President) have knowledge of how a free market works and that they make decisions based on economics. Neither of these assumptions is true. A crisis may be a reason to push through laws that have nothing to do with economics but everything to do with personal agendas. For example, politicians may be more concerned with income redistribution, consumer safety, clean energy, global warming, appeasing special interest groups, and winning the next election than they are in sound economic policies.

CAN WE LEARN FROM HISTORY?

Many of our problems stem from inadequate investments and slow growth. Sensible economics calls for business-friendly policies. We are doing the opposite. By emphasizing Keynesian policies, we are increasing the national debt and bankrupting the country. If we continue to create money, we will repeat the 1970s with higher prices and rising unemployment.

How can the government continue to borrow and spend more and more? Three things have made this possible. The government has borrowed from foreigners, the American dollar is the standard currency, and the Fed has monetized the debt.

DISTRIBUTION AND GROWTH

History has taught us that when countries pay more attention to income distribution and neglect growth, they end up with more income inequality and a diminished economy. Nations have to grow to replace goods that deteriorate over time. No country can reach a standstill because they are either growing or dying. Many politicians in Washington are obsessed with promoting fairness and income inequality. The standard prescription involves raising taxes on the wealthy, increasing the minimum wage, and expanding government benefits.

For example, in the United States, liberal states who promote fairness overgrowth experience a wider income gap between the rich and the poor than do more conservative states. The Gini coefficient measures income inequality. A Gini coefficient of zero means perfect equality of income, and a Gini coefficient of one represents perfect inequality. The US Census Bureau annually calculates the Gini coefficient for the 50 states and the District of Columbia.

According to recent Census Bureau data, the District of Columbia, New York, Connecticut, Mississippi, and Louisiana have the highest income inequality measure: while Wyoming, Alaska, Utah, Hawaii, and New Hampshire have the lowest Gini coefficients. The three most unequal places – Washington, D.C., New York, and Connecticut are the most liberal. Four of the five states with the lowest coefficient, Wyoming, Alaska, Utah, and New Hampshire, are generally conservative states.

The 19 states with the highest minimum wage have the widest income gap between rich and poor. A Cato Institute report measured the value of state welfare benefits. The report found that the higher the benefits package offered by the state, the higher the Gini coefficient indicating that raising tax rates or the minimum wage fails to achieve greater equality and may make income gaps wider. President John F. Kennedy used to say that *a rising tide lifts all boats*. His point was that there could be an increase in everyone's standard of living with sufficient growth.

SUMMARY

The one cause of inflation is an increase in the money supply and the one cause of unemployment is excessive inventories. When a business produces more goods than consumers are buying, it must cut back production. If the company continues to have a surplus problem, it will lower prices. Notice that this happens after a cut back in production. What can cause excessive inventories? Business greed and bad government policy can make a bad situation worse. Greed led to the Great Depression of the 1930s and the financial collapse of 2007-2008.

For many years, economists believed a tradeoff existed between inflation and unemployment. Inflation usually occurs when unemployment is low, and inflation is low when unemployment is high. In other words, we could bring about lower prices with more unemployment or increase employment at the expense of inflation. In the 1970s, we had these problems simultaneously, so what gives? Cost-push inflation caused the "worst of both worlds" predicament of growing inflation and unemployment in the 1970s. Cost-push inflation is not very responsive to a decline in demand. Thus typical Keynesian policies were not effective against inflation in the short-run. Prices came down eventually with a prolonged decline in demand.

Rising prices and growing unemployment pose a policy dilemma. Suppose authorities use discretionary monetary and fiscal policies to depress the economy in hopes of bringing prices down. In that case, the unemployment problem worsens without any appreciable effect on prices. If, on the other hand, the government stimulates the economy to create additional jobs, the inflation problem worsens as demand pulls prices up. All economists agree that a large part of the solution would be to revitalize the industrial base to encourage American companies to stay home. If investments in capital goods were to increase productivity, we could solve inflation and unemployment. Therefore, the best thing to do is encourage an increase in productivity by giving businesses incentives to make capital investments and spend more money on research and development.

CHAPTER 10
INTERNATIONAL TRADE

Imports are goods we buy from other countries, and exports are goods we sell to other countries. A country must export if it wants to continue importing. A continuous outlaw of money will lead to bankruptcy, even a rich one like the United States. Conversely, a constant inflow of money allows a country to buy from others indefinitely.

The US population is less than 5 percent of the world's population, yet we import most of the world's traded goods. Your shirts come from Malaysia or Bangladesh, your Levi jeans from Mexico, your Timberland shoes from Thailand, your coffee from Brazil, and your bananas from South America. Your car is from Japan. Apple assembles their phones in Shenzen, China. Our top four trading partners are Canada, China, Mexico, and Japan.

American manufacturing is more dependent on imported metals and minerals than in the past and has to import 100% of 19 strategic metals. The US has domestic resources for 18 of the 19 metals and minerals, but a maze of government regulations has made mining difficult. Without reform of the mining permit process, this situation will starve the US of the resources it needs to build everything from smartphones to weapons systems.

Companies use rare earth metals to manufacture everything from electric or hybrid vehicles, wind turbines, consumer electronics, and other clean energy technologies. The US is dependant on China for its supply of rare earth metals because China refines 80% of rare earth metals. Europe is basing its future on high-tech products and applications, but while it requires vast amounts of rare earth metals to do so, it produces next to none of these critical elements. We need rare earth minerals to manufacture the F-35 Fight Jet and other sophisticated weaponry. Lockheed Martin aircraft rely heavily on rare earths for critical components, such as electrical power systems and magnets.

Like lithium, rare earths are abundant. However, deposits large enough to make economic sense are only found in a limited number of areas worldwide, with the largest deposits discovered so far in China. Rare earth exports are a lucrative business for Asia's biggest economy, where it has virtually established world domination. And this domination is not good news for Europe—or the United States, for that matter.

America is too dependant on foreign nations for the things we need. The pandemic revealed our lack of productive capacity when we could not secure necessary materials like masks, PCR tests, and certain medicines. The US doesn't even produce shoes any longer. As long as our politicians are more concerned about the environment and social programs than economic independence, America will remain vulnerable. How long will it take a growing country five times the US's population to overtake us economically? How long can America afford to finance over 800 military bases worldwide, whereas China only has to support only one base?

RUSSIA, CHINA and EUROPE

The US used to hold almost absolute sway over NATO and EU's global politics. But now, Europe is slipping from Washington's grasp as it moves closer to the east. For the first time, China has replaced the United States as Europe's leading trading partner. America has nonetheless treated this alliance structure as an extension of its power and interests instead of being a true partnership of merits. America's hegemony, the predominance of one state or social group over others, is on its deathbed.

China has expanded its economy with its Belt and Road initiative (BRI). The belt refers to water, and the road relates to land. BRI is an ambitious economic development and commercial project that focuses on improving connectivity and cooperation among multiple countries spread across Asia, Africa, and Europe. Dubbed as the Project of the Century by the Chinese authorities, the project spans 78 countries with a network of roadways, railways, maritime ports, power grids, oil and gas pipelines.

Chinese Foreign has hailed Beijing-Moscow cooperation as playing a critical role in maintaining international stability, adding that the two nations are starting a new chapter in bilateral relations. There is a growing economic relationship between the two nations, especially with the Belt and Road Initiative and the Eurasian Economic Union.

The relationship between Russia and China grows closer with the completion of a bridge between the two countries. The first bridge linking Russia and China, suitable for automobiles and trains, is operational. The bridge is 1,700 feet and is estimated to transport 4 million metric tons of goods and 2 million Chinese tourists annually over the Amur River.

Russia and Europe's relationship grows more robust with completing the Nord Stream 2 natural gas pipeline, the second pipeline connecting Russia's rich resource to Germany and beyond. Washington sees the pipeline as a threat to its liquid natural gas exports and has placed sanctions on countries and companies who support the pipeline's construction. But European nations need a reasonably priced and reliable energy source to replace oil and nuclear power. Despite America's efforts to sabotage the project, the pipeline is all but complete.

DOMESTIC VERSUS FOREIGN LABOR

Suppose an American company can move to Mexico and pay a Mexican worker two dollars an hour or stay in America and pay an American worker twenty dollars an hour. Should the company move to Mexico? The answer is maybe yes and maybe no; the company must consider output as well as input. The company should base its decision on its labor cost per unit, not just the labor cost per hour. If the labor cost per unit is lower in America, then the company should stay in America despite higher wages.

Labor-intensive companies can save money by moving their operations offshore to take advantage of the lower wages. For example, American clothing companies pay Bangladesh senior sewing operators 35 cents an hour, $16.60 a week, and $71.94 a month. Bangladesh has about 4,000 garment factories that export mainly to the United States and Europe. International companies such as Wal-Mart, Tesco, H&M, Zara, Carrefour, Gap, Metro, J.C. Penny, Marks & Spencer, Kohl's, Levi Strauss, and Tommy Hilfiger import in bulk from Bangladesh. However, capital-intensive companies can take advantage of America's highly educated workforce, a solid infrastructure, and abundant capital.

ECONOMIES OF SCALE

When a company grows, it experiences greater economies of scale because of a reduction in its long-run average cost curve. For example, a hefty $200,000 tractor is more efficient than a small $25,000 tractor. A farmer who owns 5,000 acres of land can buy the expensive tractor, but the small farmer must use the unproductive one. If a country chooses not to trade with other nations, it is like a small farmer with limited resources. But if it trades with other nations, its resources are greatly expanded. For example, Boeing Aircraft could not produce its 747 jumbo jets if it could not sell the aircraft internationally because the American market is too small to justify the huge costs.

ABSOLUTE ADVANTAGE

If it a country can produce a good with fewer resources than other countries, it has an absolute advantage. Because land, labor, capital, and entrepreneurship differ from country to country, each country has an absolute advantage in something. For example, Brazil has an absolute advantage in coffee due to its climate and geography; likewise, the United States has an absolute advantage in wheat due to its farm land.

COMPARATIVE ADVANTAGE

Now, suppose that America had an absolute advantage in producing handmade wicker baskets. Does this mean we should spend time making baskets? The answer is no because of high opportunity costs. In other words, if we were to spend time producing baskets, our opportunity cost would be less devotion to technology. A country has a comparative advantage if it can produce a product with lower opportunity costs than other nations.

BARRIERS TO TRADE

Countries prosper if they produce with a comparative advantage and practice free trade. So, why do we have trade restrictions? Before we answer this question, let's look at how nations restrict trade.

Tariffs and Quotas

Although there are gains from international specialization and exchange, most countries restrict trade to some extent. Tariffs and quotas restrict international trade. A tariff is a tax levied against an import, and a quota sets a maximum quantity of a good that a country can import. If specialization takes advantage of comparative advantage, why do countries restrict trade? Restrictions benefit certain producers that lobby their governments for these benefits. For example, US textile manufacturers have benefitted from legislation restricting textile imports, thereby raising US textile prices. These higher prices hurt the domestic consumer, but consumers are usually unaware of the situation. Trade restrictions interfere with the free flow of products across borders and tend to hurt the overall economy. Tariffs are revenue-enhancing, but the main reason for trade restrictions is protection. When foreigners have to pay a tariff, they tend to raise prices to make up for the increased cost, giving the domestic country a price advantage, everything else being equal.

Relative Tax Rates

Most countries tax domestic companies according to where they earn their income, making homegrown companies globally competitive. The US is a rare exception because it taxes US companies at its corporate rate if they decide to repatriate income earned abroad. For example, if the Dutch-based Unilever makes money in Ireland and brings the money back to Holland, it pays the lower Irish corporate rate. If America's Pfizer Corporation earns money in Ireland, it pays the Irish tax, plus a US tax when it brings this money back home. Thus, US corporate giants prefer to keep their foreign earnings abroad.

WHY TRADE RESTRICTIONS?

Free and open trade provides the most significant efficiencies and the highest living standards for almost everyone. So why are tariffs and quotas imposed? Some of the following reasons for trade restrictions are valid, some are not, and some are valid only for certain countries.

National Defense

War makes countries vulnerable to embargos. If the enemy restricts the flow of necessary war supplies, a country will lose its ability to continue the conflict. Israel is a country surrounded by enemies. Even though it may not have a comparative advantage in guns, it would still produce them.

Protect Jobs

American companies can justify almost any protectionist policy. Congress has an incentive to protect special interest groups because the saved jobs are visible, whereas the jobs lost are not obvious. Even the unemployed workers may not know that they are losing their jobs because of protective tariffs.

A "beggar-my-neighbor" policy is when a country is attempting to push its unemployment problems off onto its neighbor. When we restrict Americans from buying foreign products, foreign unemployment increases, and they will buy less from us. Moreover, if this happens, foreigners may retaliate by imposing restrictions against American products. The result is higher prices, lower quantity, and a reduction in living standards for all. We call this back and forth exchange among countries a "tariff war," and no one wins a tariff war.

Comparative Advantage

Because of high wages and a highly capitalized economy, the US should concentrate on capital-intensive products and not labor-intensive.

A Nation Can Restrict Trade

Developing countries who are dependent on a few exports should impose trade restrictions to help diversify their economies. But a nation like the US that is already very diversified should practice free trade.

Protect Infant Industries

Just as adults need to protect babies, governments need to protect infant industries until they can compete independently. A foreign competitor may have the advantages of established markets and economies of scale, putting the domestic company at a disadvantage. This infant industry policy may be compelling for a small developing country, but consider the following. First, how do we know that smallness was the only disadvantage? Even after the companies grow, the foreign companies may still have advantages. Second, at what point do we stop protecting the infant industry?

Protection from Dumping

Companies may be able to price their products below cost in some cases, a practice economists call dumping. For example, the Commerce Department has dismissed charges lodged by producers of Florida fruit and vegetables of dumping by Mexican growers during the winter season. The Department of Commerce ruled in favor of Mexico because vegetables are perishable—all growers sell below cost at some point in the season and make it up in others. Selling at prices below costs can be a standard practice and is not necessarily dumping.

EXCHANGE RATES

The lack of a common currency complicates trade among nations. How many dollars does it take to buy a shirt from India or television from China? To facilitate trade among countries, we need a market for foreign exchange. Foreign exchange is a foreign currency needed to carry out international transactions. The supply and demand for foreign exchange come together in foreign exchange markets to determine the equilibrium exchange rate. The exchange measures the price of one currency in terms of another. For example, the exchange rate between the yen and the dollar might indicate that it takes $1.04 to equal one yen's value. The exchange rate affects the price of imports and exports and allows for nations to trade. The values of all currencies are determined by the forces of demand and supply of that currency on the world market.

Suppose you had a net worth of ten million dollars. Where is the best place to keep your money? The following factors influence the demand for currencies around the world.

- What kind of return can you make on your money? If interest rates are higher in the United States than in Germany, you may decide to keep your money in America and not Germany.

• The inflation rate is the next thing to consider. If you hold your money in American dollars for a year and the United States has an inflation rate of 8 percent, then each dollar has lost 8 percent in value. So, you want to keep your money in a country with a low inflation rate.

• You should keep your money in a country that is economically and politically stable.

The American dollar is the world's standard reserve currency. When countries trade among one another, they will convert their currencies to dollars and then trade on a dollar per dollar basis instead of using their own currencies in exchange. Even though the euro is the second largest traded currency next to the American dollar, a European company still must convert euros to dollars for many international transactions. But this special privilege of the dollar is waning as a standard, and countries are finding alternative means to trade among one another.

Some of the biggest economies have been making alternative agreements; for example, China, and other emerging powers such as Russia, have been quietly making agreements to move away from the US dollar in international trade over the past few years. The second-largest economy on earth (China) and the third-largest economy on the planet (Japan) struck a deal that will promote the use of their currencies (rather than the US dollar) when trading with each other. China and the United Arab Emirates have agreed to ditch the US dollar and use their currencies in oil transactions. These actions will have profound effects on the American economy.

Because much of the world needs the dollar to trade with other nations, the dollar's demand remains high, and thus the value of the dollar remains high, allowing a high standard of living for Americans. If the dollar falls from its perch as the world's standard currency, Americans will lose much of their buying power as the dollar loses value. The dollar will lose value because the demand for the dollar will decline in the world market.

Economists use the term float to describe the process of demand and supply in determining the value of currencies. However, almost all countries practice what we call a "dirty" float to influence their currencies' demand and supply. When countries compete with one another by lowering their currency's value to give them a competitive edge, economists call this conflict a currency war. When a country's currency falls in value, its products become less expensive to foreigners, selling more. Everyone loses over the long run.

China directly affects the US dollar by loosely pegging the value of its currency, the renminbi, to the dollar. China's central bank uses a modified version of a traditional fixed exchange rate that differs from the United States and many other countries' floating exchange rates. Thus, they can influence trade by changing the Yuan's value relative to the dollar. If China wants to increase its exports, it can set the Yuan's value lower, making Chinese products less expensive to anyone using American dollars. The US Congress may retaliate against the Chinese if it believes the Chinese are rigging the game in their favor.

CURRENCY WARS

Investors tend to gravitate toward pro-growth sensitive assets. For example, if investors lose confidence in a country's currency, that currency's value will fall as demand declines. European countries are in trouble because they have expanded their welfare systems, shortened the workweek, and paid government workers generously while borrowing more and turning to creative financing forms rather than raising taxes. These policies have led to a debt crisis that is spreading across the globe.

Some countries have responded to this crisis by devaluing their currencies. When the value of a country's currency decreases, its products become less expensive to foreigners, promoting increased growth and jobs. When a government takes steps to influence the demand and supply of its currency on the international market, currency values change. Currency wars represent what economists call a zero-sum game. That is, the game yields winners and losers.

The Federal Reserve embarked on a massive bond-buying program with newly created money starting in 2012, something the Fed calls quantitative easing. Quantitative easing devalues the dollar because of the increase in the supply of dollars on the international market. However, a decline in the dollar's value means an appreciation of foreign currencies in relative terms, which puts foreigners at a trade disadvantage. Throughout history, this conflict between countries has led to currency wars.

BALANCE OF PAYMENTS ADJUSTMENTS

The balance of trade concerns the flow of money in and out of a country via trade. But there are other ways money can enter or leave a country other than imports and exports. For example, when Americans travel abroad and spend money, money leaves America, but money enters America when foreigners travel in the US. When foreigners buy in America, money comes in. When Americans purchase stock or land in foreign countries, dollars leave. The term balance of payments refers to the total quantity of money entering or leaving a country.

In the long run, countries want neither a persistent and highly favorable balance surplus nor a deficit. Inflation results when the balance of payments is too favorable over an extended time. On the other hand, if we have a severe payments deficit, unemployment could worsen. However, in the long run, the money entering will tend to equal money leaving, having a payment surplus in some years and a payments deficit in others. How is this?

A freely flexible international exchange-rate system will automatically correct a balance of payments problem for a country. For example, suppose that the US has a payments deficit with too much money leaving the country. The dollar's value will decrease with an increase in supply, making foreign goods more expensive for Americans and American goods cheaper for foreigners. A reversal occurs when Americans buy less from foreigners, and foreigners buy more from Americans. Now, what happens if America experiences a payments surplus? With more dollars entering the country than dollars leaving the country, the global market's supply decreases, increasing its value. When the dollar rises in value, Americans will purchase more from foreigners, and foreigners will buy less from America. There is a tendency over the long run for there to be a balance in the balance of payments. The amount of money entering a nation tends to equal the amount leaving a nation over time.

INTERNATIONAL MONETARY FUND

Countries with a balance of payments problem can borrow money from the International Monetary Fund (IMF) through Special Drawing Rights (SDRs), which is an entity made up of five currencies, including the US dollar, the euro, the Chinese renminbi, the Japanese yen, and the British pound sterling. SDRs could become the world's standard currency for international settlements.

Special Drawing Rights work like this. Suppose the value of the dollar were to plummet. The US government could then approach other countries, such as Germany and Japan, and request that the IMF transfer United States SDRs to those countries' accounts. In return, Germany and Japan would supply the United States with euros and yen. The United States could then use the euros and yen to buy dollars worldwide, thus increasing the dollar's value compared with the euro and yen. Economists call this chain of events a dirty float. Some form of SDR could replace the dollar as the world's standard currency.

A STABLE DOMESTIC ECONOMY

Only stable economies will result in stable currencies over the long run regardless of what countries do in the short run. If a country experiences persistent high inflation rates and is unstable, foreigners will flee that currency for safer and more stable currencies, gold, silver, or bitcoin.

SUMMARY

Despite the many advantages of free trade, trade restrictions are the norm because they do the following:

- national defense reasons.
- protect specific domestic jobs.
- protect from cheap foreign labor.
- diversify a country's economy.
- protect infant industries.
- protect from dumping.

Inflation can result because of trade barriers. These higher costs may diminish the producer's ability to compete with foreign companies because of higher domestic prices. For example, many American companies find it difficult to compete globally with sugar products because sugar is so much more expensive in the United States than anywhere else in the world.

International trade requires exchanging currencies in the global exchange market according to current exchange rates, and market forces of demand and supply determine exchange rates. If the need for a currency increases compared with the international market supply, that currency's value will increase. If the demand for a currency declines relative to the supply, the currency's value will decline. A clean float occurs when the laws of supply and demand determine values and a "dirty float" occurs when countries interfere with market forces. Alternatively, some countries peg the value of their currencies to another currency. If the US has an unemployment problem, we want the value of the dollar to decline. If inflation is the problem, we want the value of the dollar to increase.

Because of the effects of international trade on employment and prices, a country should have a balance in its balance of payments over the long run. If a country experiences a favorable balance of payments problem over an extended time, the large influx of money could cause inflation. We experience unemployment with long-term payments deficit.

A perfectly free international monetary system is self-adjusting over time. If a country is experiencing either inflation or unemployment, the forces of demand and supply of its currency will adjust to alleviate the problem. Over the long run, money leaving a country tends to equal money entering.

CHAPTER 11
BUSINESS CYCLES

All advanced industrial economies face swings in economic activity from euphoric highs, which economists call expansions, to catastrophic lows, which economists call recessions or depressions. This ebb and flow of economic activity is the business cycle. Whether we are talking about communism or capitalism and every type of system in between, the business cycle is ever-present. In many ways, the term business cycle is misleading because it implies a regularity in the timing and duration of upswings and downswings. However, expansions and recessions occur at irregular intervals and last for varying lengths of time.

TWO WORLD VIEWS

America used to have a lot of small forest fires. Because this was a concern, the government embarked on fire prevention programs for the nation's forests. These programs eliminated many would-be fires. So, we experienced fewer small fires, but we had larger fires when a fire broke out. Officials realized that the small forest fires helped burn away the undergrowth and deadwood without actually reaching the mature trees and the deep forest. By preventing small fires, the undergrowth and deadwood were allowed to accumulate. The underbrush acted as fuel to fires, spreading them further into the forests while destroying many older mature trees. The lesson here is that nature is better off not disturbed.

Austrians believe the same way about free markets and government intervention. They even propose that periods of depression are just a cycle in a healthy economy, similar to forest fires. In the aftermath of a depression, new business opportunities and industries will emerge, and this is how capitalism and business cycles occur. On the other hand, Keynesians have always advocated rules, laws, and taxes to guide the economy to a full-employment equilibrium. Austrians believe seeking full-employment equilibrium is an elusive goal in controlled economies.

Austrians differ from Keynesians in the basic approach to solving economic problems. Austrians believe that nature should be allowed to run its course. The business cycle's ups and downs are inevitable, and the government should not interfere with this natural mechanism. On the other hand, Keynesians believe that Governments should intervene in markets to control the ups and downs of the business cycle. Keynesians believe that policies can be best formulated by econometric models that aid policymakers in making decisions. Austrians believe that government mandates are more reactive than pro-active. Instead of concentrating on long-term growth, it forces authorities to dwell on the short-run.

DEMAND MANAGEMENT ECONOMICS

The Great Depression was fertile ground for the ideas of

John M. Keynes. The Employment Act of 1946 empowered the federal government to pursue maximum employment, production, and purchasing power. The 1978 Humphrey Hawkins Act (the Full-employment and Balanced Growth Act) laid out the mandate's specifics.

President John F. Kennedy

Although we had recessions in 1948-1949, 1953-1954, and 1957-1958, it was not until the recession of 1960-1961 that the government used fiscal policies to control the economy. In 1961, President Kennedy asked Congress to approve a tax cut without a corresponding decrease in government spending. This idea was new to Congress, and it took them two years to approve a tax cut. The Keynesian practice of fine-tuning the economy, guiding the economy through monetary and fiscal policies became widely accepted after 1961.

FOUR PHASES OF THE BUSINESS CYCLE

Business cycles have four phases. When the economy reaches the end of its expansionary period, we say it has peaked. After the peak, the economy slides into a recession and eventually reaches a trough, which is the bottom. After the trough, business activity picks up, and the economy recovers.

Consumption Sector

Nondurable goods are goods consumers consume within a short time, such as food. Durable goods have a long life span, such as automobiles. Consumer demand for nondurable goods is more stable than for durable goods. When your income declines, you will still buy food, but you will not purchase a new car. Consumer demand tends to be steady over time. As revenues fall, we try to maintain our spending habits for as long as possible. We are loath to give up things that we have been accustomed to having. Economists define savings as money earned but not spent, such as money in a savings account. Real savings occur when you own something that has a market value, such as a boat. Dissaving means taking money out of savings. During difficult times we try to maintain our lifestyles by dissaving. Thus the consumption sector is the most stable sector of gross domestic product.

Investment Sector

Whereas the consumption sector is the most stable, the investment sector is the most unstable. Investors will make decisions based on what they think will happen in the future, and these expectations can easily change. Negative expectations and uncertainty can nix investment decisions in the bud. Fear and uncertainty are the twin killers of investment.

Interest rates alone do not determine the level of investment. Will a decrease in interest rates lead to an increase in investments? The answer could be yes if the expected rate of return supersedes the cost of paying interest. But the answer could be no if the anticipated rate of return is less than the interest expense. In other words, the effect of a change in interest rates on investments is relative.

Government Sector

Economists compare the plight of policymakers to that of a helmsman, a captain of an ocean liner. Imagine yourself as the captain of this ship headed across the ocean from New York City to London. Rough weather has thrown you off course, and you find yourself headed too far north, so you turn the wheel to the right, but the momentum of the ship carries you too far to the south, forcing you to turn the wheel to the left. Now the momentum heads the ship too far to the north again. This pattern continues as you zigzag across the Atlantic Ocean.

Foreign Sector

The foreign sector can have a counter-cyclical or a pro-cyclical influence on the economy. The foreign sector is counter-cyclical when it moderates the business cycle's ups and downs, cushioning inflation or unemployment. For example, suppose there are inflationary pressures due to an increase in aggregate demand. Without the foreign sector, this increase in demand would bear heavily on the domestic economy and feed inflation flames. However, if a portion of the demand increase is for foreign products, there is less inflation at home.

The foreign sector can be pro-cyclical. The more we trade with foreign nations, the more external events affect what happens here in America. For example, if Greece, Italy, Spain, or Portugal declares bankruptcy, the American economy suffers. Expanded trade makes us more vulnerable to the global business cycle. A boom in China will stimulate our economy and vice versa. When foreign economies prosper, everyone benefits.

FISCAL POLICIES & STABILIZERS

Discretionary fiscal policies and automatic stabilizers differ. Most economists agree that automatic stabilizers, such as unemployment benefits, positively affect the economy. When unemployment increases, more people receive unemployment benefits, thus cushioning the decline in consumer demand. No one has to make a policy decision for this to happen; it happens automatically. Therefore, automatic stabilizers tend to smooth out the business cycle's swings because they have a counter-cyclical effect on the economy.

CRASH OF 2007 -2008

Being over-leveraged can cause a collapse. If a bank has one million dollars and borrows 30 million dollars to invest, we say that the bank is leveraged 30 to 1. If the asset increases in value, the bank's profits multiply by a factor of 30. However, if the investment declines in value, losses are multiplied by a factor of 30. It was common for banks to be leveraged 30 to 1 leading up to the 2007-2008 crash.

A great book on the subject is *Fool's Gold* by Gillian Tett. Following is a quote from the book's preface:

> *Were the bankers mad? Were they evil? Or were they simply grotesquely greedy? The 2007-2008 credit boom is a story of how an entire financial system went wrong due to flawed incentives within banks and investment funds and the rating agencies, and warped regulatory structures.*

By 2006, individuals, businesses, banks, and highly leveraged governments incurred losses when debtors defaulted on their loans. Within months, hundreds of billions of dollars of assets vanished. By late 2007, consumer and business spending was down, and the recession ensued. By 2008, this realization of vanishing assets spread around the globe, culminating in a financial panic.

Federal Reserve Takes Action in 2008

The Fed took action in 2008 to stem the tide of growing unemployment. In 2008, the rapidly eroding confidence in the financial system caused significant financial firms to collapse. Fearing that these conditions could usher in another great depression, the Fed took action to stem the tide. For the first time in history, the Fed began lending money to nonbank corporations. The Fed also started purchasing assets from Fannie Mae and Freddie Mac. Then the Fed agreed to exchange billions of dollars of risk-free federal bonds for billions of dollars of high-risk private bonds held by corporations.

Too Big to Fail or Too Big to Save?

Do bailouts stabilize the business cycle? Keynesians support bailouts because they believe that corporate failures could lead to economic collapse. Austrians believe that bailouts inhibit the economy's self-adjusting mechanism. GM routinely agreed to generous labor contracts with the United Auto Workers union (UAW). By the time the 2007-2008 recession hit, GM was uncompetitive due to high labor costs, including high pension costs. In previous times, the company would have declared bankruptcy, and the bankruptcy courts would have sorted out who gets what.

The government gave GM money and allowed it to exist with all its baggage intact. This type of bailout privatizes gains while socializing losses leaving you and me to pick up the tab. Believing that the government will not allow them to fail, banks continued reckless activity. This moral hazard influenced every large corporation that the government saved, including Chrysler, Citicorp, Goldman Sachs, AIG, and many others. Thus, we no longer have a competitive marketplace.

The recession of 2007-2008 has ushered in something called industrial policy. President Obama claimed in 2009 that the government must make strategic decisions about strategic industries. The government has earmarked billions of dollars supporting favored industries, such as renewable energy. The United States has restructured health care, financial services, and the energy sector.

The great recession of 2007-2008 was the worst since the Great Depression of the 1930s. Because of its severity and the Federal Reserve's expanded role, the Fed has reshaped credit markets on a grand scale. These events have moved us further away from a free market system because Congress has learned nothing from the great recession.

RULES vs. PRINCIPLES

We have become a nation of rules where rules rule and not

people. In this world of rules, no human being is in charge—we are all subject to the law—and regulations are almost impossible to change. The rule-makers may retire or die, but the rules live, and everyone is subject to the letter of the law. Meanwhile, the system is inflexible.

Philip K. Howard describes our current state of affairs in his book *The Rule of Nobody—Saving America from Dead Laws and Broken Government*. He describes the economy as being tied down like Gulliver was in Jonathan Swift's classic book *Gulliver's Travels*. *The Rule of Nobody* explains the general decay we are experiencing. New, mobile institutions languish on the drawing board, while old ones are not reformed and tended. Executives at public agencies are robbed of discretionary power because court judgments and regulations bind their hands. Howard argues for returning to the framers' vision of public law—setting goals and boundaries, not dictating daily choices. The book explains how America went wrong and offers a guide to liberate human ingenuity. Mindless rigidity has descended upon the land, from the schoolhouse to the White House and even your house. Nothing much works because no one is free to make things work.

Howard's ideas are similar to Friedrich Hayek's ideas. The main point to Hayek's book *The Road to Serfdom* is the loss of individual liberty when planners realize that the only way for the plan to work is to mandate that everyone adhere to the program. Thus the road to serfdom is complete. Hayek warns that strict adherence to a centralized plan undermines the virtues of a free society. The virtues lost are:

- Independence.
- The successful reliance on voluntary activity.
- Noninterference with one's neighbor.
- A healthy suspicion of power and authority.

SUMMARY

Change is inevitable, and the boom and bust cycle of the economy is a natural process. The consumption sector helps stabilize the economy, while the investment sector causes volatility. Interest rates can decline, but if investors are pessimistic, low-interest rates may not increase investments. To increase investments, investors have to be confident about the future.

The multiplication process takes place when money changes hands. The accelerator occurs when spending increase leads to secondary investments. The money spent on a new highway will lead to more motels, restaurants, gas stations, etc. This multiplication process affects the business cycle in unpredictable ways. Slow but steady growth is better than booms and busts.

A lack of knowledge may accentuate the business cycle. How can we expect policymakers to make the right decisions if they do not understand the problem? Lag effects lesson the effectiveness of fiscal policies. The recognition lag, decision lag, and action lag tend to make any policy pro-cyclical rather than counter-cyclical, and automatic stabilizers are more beneficial than discretionary fiscal policies.

The foreign sector complicates monetary and fiscal decisions. Foreign wars, revolutions, lousy weather, bankruptcies, oil spills, and big business actions pose a nightmare for policymakers. For example, what happens if Iran blocks the flow of oil through the Strait of Hormuz? The Strait of Hormuz is only 21 miles at its narrowest point, and it is the world's most crucial oil-trade route. Another problem with monetary and fiscal policies is that other considerations may be more important than growth. Goals of national defense, equity, minimizing negative externalities, redistributing the wealth, fairness, or only looking good for the next election may take precedence over stability and growth.

CHAPTER 12
CRISES of 2007 – 2008

The financial crises of 2007–2008 could be a spy novel; it is a story of intrigue, under-the-table dealings mystery, excessive pride, ambition, and greed. It is a story of epic battles where heroes are villains and villains are heroes. Congress laid the foundation of the financial collapse of 2007 and 2008 by encouraging banks to relax their lending standards for home mortgages to achieve their goal of increasing homeownership, especially among low-income households. Simultaneously, Congress put pressure on Fannie Mae and Freddie Mac to lower their standards to purchase more subprime loans from banks, allowing a record number of Americans to fall into debt. The downturn escalated when people abandoned their houses while refusing to make payments. The increase in subprime loans also increased banks' risk, forcing them to find ways to shift the risk onto someone else. Thus the system gave birth to collateralized debt obligations (CDOs).

A collateralized debt obligation is a complex financial product backed by a pool of loans and other assets and sold to institutional investors. A CDO is a particular type of derivative because, as its name implies, some underlying asset determines its value. To create a CDO, banks gather cash flow-generating assets—such as mortgages, bonds, and other types of debt—and repackage them into discrete classes or tranches based on the investors' credit risk level. For example, if mortgages are put into the CDO, low-risk loans will pay lower interest than high-risk mortgages. The higher interest for risky loans is meant to give the investor an incentive to take more risk when purchasing the CDO.

A collateralized debt obligation is an asset pool made up of mortgages, bonds, and other loan types. For example, investors can package subprime mortgages into a CDO. Investors name CDO's according to the type of underlying asset within the CDO. For example, mortgage-backed securities (MBS) contain mortgages, and asset-backed securities (ABS) contain corporate debt, auto loans, or credit card debt. Investors call CDOs "collateralized" because the returns of the underlying assets, people making payments on the mortgages, etc., are the collateral that gives the CDO value. If borrowers quit making their monthly payments, the CDO loses value.

The more a bank keeps in reserve, the less it has to lend out and thus less profit to the bank. One day, a group of bankers was sitting around a pool in Boca Ratan, Florida, brainstorming how to convince the Fed to lower their reserve requirements. They came up with the idea that would lessen their risk level.

The idea the bankers formalized to lower their risk level was the Credit Default Swap (CDS), which is similar to insurance against default. A default occurs when borrowers quit making their monthly payments on a loan. This is how a CDS works. Banks pay someone, for example, Goldman Sachs, to assume the default risk. If a default occurred on the bonds (meaning people quit making their payments on the loan), the CDS seller, such as Goldman Sachs, would suffer the loss and pay the bank to make up for the money it lost by borrowers defaulting on their loans. Thus the CDS swapped the risk of default from one party to another party, from a bank to another entity. When banks took this idea to the Fed in hopes that the Fed would lower their reserve requirements, the ploy worked.

But the story does not end with the birth of credit default swaps. Two parties form a synthetic collateralized debt obligation by making a bet on a CDO's outcome. The first party will bet that a default will occur, and the second party bets that default will not happen. Using derivatives, banks created many synthetic CDOs using the same mortgage securities, all of which would rise or fall in value depending on how the mortgages were performing.

DERIVATIVES MARKET

Because no one can predict the future for sure, complicated mathematical models help participants in the derivatives market agree on an asset's future value; economists call this prediction of future value notional value. When person A enters into a futures contract (sometimes called a forward contract) with person B, we call this practice hedging. A hedge fund is a fund that uses the futures market in its portfolio, a mix of different types of investments.

The following hypothetical case would never happen, but it will give you an idea of how the derivative market works. Let's suppose you and I make a bet on the weather a month from now. Will it rain or not on a specific date? I forecast that it is going to rain, and you say that it will be a sunny day. A week after we make our contract, someone offers to purchase your derivative, your contract, with me. They are willing to give you money betting that the sun will shine on the specified agreed-upon date. They relieve you of the contract you had with person A, and they take your place. If they bet correctly, they receive payment from person A, and if they bet wrongly, they pay person A.

An over-the-counter-derivative is an agreement between two parties, and only the two parties are privy to the terms of the contract. Even the purchaser of the derivative may not be privy to the facts. Let's say you are the treasurer of a city, and a salesperson from Bear Stearns Investment Bank calls you (Bear is now a part of JP Morgan Chase Bank). He asks if you are interested in buying a security with a triple-A rating that has a history of 25% return. Because Bear Stearns has an excellent reputation and the security has the highest credit rating, you take the deal without knowing the particulars.

BROOKSLEY BORN

This story begins with Brooksley Born, the Commodity Futures Trading Commission (CFTC) chairperson, the federal agency that oversees the futures and commodity options markets, from August 1996 to June 1999. The government authorized the CFTC to detect fraud in the over-the-counter derivatives market.

When she looked into the market, she became concerned about the dangers it posed for the entire economy. From her vantage point as chair of the Commodity Futures Trading Commission, she was aware of how quickly the over-the-counter derivatives market was growing and how little federal regulators knew about it. The notional value of the derivative's market was about $600 trillion!

Brooksley saw the danger in the market, including fraud and speculation. One example is Orange County, California, which went bankrupt because of high-risk bets in the derivatives market. These failures alarmed Brooksley because few in government knew about derivatives, though banks were dealers in the market. Her concern was that a default in the market could cause a domino effect throughout the economy. Things came to a head when Proctor & Gamble, who ended up owing $200 billion in the derivatives market, sued their derivative dealer, Bankers Trust, for fraud, alleging that the bank had convinced them to purchase complex derivatives without proper explanation. In 1996, Bankers Trust settled with Proctor & Gamble, forgiving most of the debt. This court case helped shed light on the derivative's market.

Now here is where things get interesting. When Brooksley contacted the Treasury Department, the Federal Reserve, and the Securities and Exchange Commission about her concerns, not only were they complacent, but they also questioned whether Brooksley and the Commodity Futures Trading Commission had the authority to take action. The government even banned the CFTC from dealing with the derivatives market.

ALAN GREENSPAN

So why was Alan Greenspan, who was Chairman of the Federal Reserve, opposed to any oversight of the derivative's market? Because Alan Greenspan is a disciple of Ayn Rand, who wrote the book, *Atlas Shrugged* in 1957. Rand believed that the market should be free of all government regulations. Here we have the Federal Reserve Chairman, responsible for regulating the banking system, opposed to any form of code. When Brooksley had a private conversation with Alan Greenspan and pointed out the extensive fraud in the derivatives market, he responded that the CFTC should not persecute fraud because it would take care of it!

DERIVATIVES MARKET

Farmers have used the concept of hedging for thousands of years. Let's suppose you are a farmer, and you decide to plant corn in early spring. However, your corn will not be ready to sell until the fall. What do you do? You can hedge your risk against a low market price in the fall by entering into a future contract with a bank. In the agreement, you agree to sell your corn at a specified price on a specified date. If the market price is less than the specified price, you gain by selling your corn at a higher price. Suppose the market price is greater than the target price, the bank gains when it sells the corn at a higher price. All markets, such as energy, precious metals, and foreign currencies, use this practice of hedging against future events.

Long Term Capital had leveraged its bets in the derivatives market with borrowed money, bet wrong, and faced bankruptcy in 1998 when it had only $4 billion in assets to fund a $1.25 trillion investment. To prevent a possible systemic collapse, big banks stepped in to rescue the firm. The banks told Congress that the LTCM problem was the exception to the rule and was not indicative of the derivative market. Congress accepted this argument and passed the Commodity Futures Modernization Act of 2000, which stripped the Commodity Futures Trading Commission of all responsibility for the derivatives market and forbid the Securities and Exchange Commission (SEC) and state regulators to interfere with over-the-counter derivatives.

Commercial banks using depositors' money to make risky investments contributed to the Great Depression of the 1930s. Consequently, Congress passed the Glass-Steagall Act in 1933, which separated commercial banks from investment banks by allowing the government to regulate commercial banks but not investment banks, thus protecting depositors while allowing wealthy individuals to take risks when dealing with investment banks.

Investment banks were making massive amounts of money in the derivatives market in the 1990s, and commercial banks wanted a piece of the action. The Glass-Steagall Act prevented them from this activity, so they petitioned Congress to change the law. Consequently, Congress passed the Private Securities Litigation Act of 1995, which protected Wall Street and banks from legal suits. Then Congress passed the Financial Services Modernization Act in 1999, which severed the differences between commercial banks and investment banks. As a result of these two acts, commercial banks were once again permitted to put depositors' money at risk as they did in the 1920s. Additionally, the

FDIC granted investors' accounts at investment banks the same protection as depositors at commercial banks, which permanently severed the distinction between investment and commercial banks.

EXCESSIVE LEVERAGE

In its simplest form, a credit default swap is a bet on a future event. Let's suppose Bank A lends one million dollars to XYZ Company. To hedge against a possible default – the possibility that XYZ Company does not pay the money back – Bank A buys credit default swap protection from ABC Corporation. Bank A agrees to pay ABC Corporation $1,000 a month, or a percentage, for five years, and if XYZ Company defaults on the loan, ABC pays Bank A one million dollars.

Joe Cassano was the head of the AIG Financial Products Division from 2001 to 2008. In theory, credit default swaps make a lot of sense, but terrible things happen when investors use too much leverage. Cassano sold billions of dollars' worth of protection to banks without having assets to support the agreements. Cassano also sold naked credit default swaps, in which two parties bet on whether there will be a default or not even though neither party holds the underlying loan. These agreements swapped the risk of default from third parties to AIG. Cassano sold $500 billion worth of credit default swaps, with at least $64 billion of that tied to the subprime mortgage market. When the financial panic broke out in 2007 with massive defaults, AIG needed a government bailout to avoid bankruptcy.

Another example of excessive leverage is Barings Bank. Barings Bank, founded in 1762, was the oldest merchant bank in

London, England. The bank was successful, well-established, and conservative. Despite its solid foundation, a rogue derivatives trader in the Singapore office, Nick Leeson, bankrupted the bank. Nick Leeson was responsible for arbitrage, buying futures contracts on one market and simultaneously selling them in another market at a higher price. The margins on arbitrage trading are small because so many investors try to take advantage of price differences, so trades have to be exceptionally large. Leeson had bought contracts in one market and held on to the agreements, betting that futures contracts would increase in the Japanese market. When the Japanese market continued to move against him, he falsified trading records to make it look profitable. An earthquake in Japan sent future prices ever lower, exacerbating his losses. Authorities declared Barings insolvent in February of 1995 when a Dutch bank bought Barings for one pound.

Another example of excessive leverage occurred with JP Morgan Bank and Bruno Iksil, a London-based trader in JP Morgan's Chief Investment Office, in May 2012. The financial community called Iksil the London Whale, or the Caveman, because he pursued trades that rivals sometimes thought were overly aggressive but often led to immense profits. In 2011, Iksil sold Credit Default Swaps (CDSs) against companies that were a part of an index – betting that they would not default on their loans. He was so confident that the value of his bet approached $100 billion back in April of 2012. Other people in the market thought Iksil was overconfident, so they bought credit default swaps on the Index. On Nov. 29, 2011, AMR Corp., American Airlines' parent company and one of the Index companies, filed for bankruptcy protection. JP Morgan had to ante-up about $2 billion to the people who bought the credit default swaps.

INVESTMENT BANKS

The government established the Securities and Exchange Commission (SEC) in 1934 as a critical reform resulting from the stock market crash of 1929. In 2004, the SEC abolished its "debt-to-net-capital rule" in favor of a voluntary process that allowed investment banks to devise their own "rule." Under this new scheme, the SEC allowed large investment banks to find their levels of risk based on their risk management computer models. Instead of adhering to the previous 12:1 debt to capital ratio, the new standard became a 40:1 ratio.

A 40:1 debt to capital ratio made huge profits possible. Still, when the economy went south in 2007, this excessive leverage led to the collapse of five investment banks: Bear Stearns, Goldman Sachs, Morgan Stanley, Merrill Lynch, and Lehman Brothers. At this time, in September 2008, the crises became a financial meltdown of epic proportions. To justify bailing out investment banks, the Federal Reserve allowed these investment banks to purchase commercial banks. Thus, the Fed granted them holding bank status; a bank holding company has all commercial banks' protections.

THE SUBPRIME MORTGAGE CRISES

The easy money policies of the Federal Reserve during the 1990s, the deregulation mania, and excessive leverage resulted in a bubble during the 2000s. Now add some greed to the mix, throw in some hubris, mix it all up with stupidity, and a massive collapse results. So why did the bubble burst so quickly? A critical factor in the mortgage collapse was the abundance of adjustable-rate mortgages issued from 2000 to 2008. Adjustable-rate mortgages begin with low-interest rates, called teaser rates, and increase yearly according to a fixed schedule. This practice fostered an increase in defaults.

Many adjustable-rate mortgages were risky subprime loans, loans made with very lenient due diligence. When the housing market collapsed in 2007-2008, and housing prices declined, many homeowners with subprime loans found themselves upside down on their mortgage, owing more on a house than it was worth on the market. The abundance of adjustable-rate mortgages and risky subprime loans made a horrible situation worse.

Banks were obligated to lend money to low-income people in their communities as mandated by the Housing and Community Reinvestment Act of 1977 (CRA). As initially enacted in 1977, the CRA required regulators to consider whether banks served their communities' needs. The government loosely enforced the law until 1993, when Congress became concerned that banks were discriminating against minorities. In 1995, regulators formulated new rules that required banks to make a certain number of loans to low and moderate-income borrowers. The new regulations also required using innovative or flexible lending practices to address credit needs.

To make it easier for banks to meet the Housing and Community Reinvestment Act mandates, Congress came up with another scheme involving the two government-sponsored enterprises, Fannie Mae and Freddie Mac. In 1992, Congress amended Fannie Mae and Freddie Mac's charter, forcing them to purchase more mortgages from banks that originated from moderate-income families. In 1999, Congress mandated Fan and Fred to increase their purchases of loans from banks that stemmed from distressed inner-city areas. Additionally, Congress pressured financial institutions in the primary mortgage market to reduce their lending standards, causing the number of sub-prime loans that Fan and Fred purchased from banks to increase.

These policies did not initially cause problems but had exasperated the economic downturn beginning in 2007. When millions of homeowners defaulted on their mortgages in 2007 and 2008, Fannie and Freddie lost billions. Consequently, they relinquished their quasi-government status and reverted to complete government control in 2008. Fannie and Freddie have been so aggressive in their mortgage buying that they now own most mortgages in America.

Politicians have spent years arguing that private lenders created the housing boom and bust and that Fannie Mae and Freddie Mac came along for the ride, which is fiction. Now thanks to the unlikely source, the Securities and Exchange Commission, we have a trail of evidence showing how the failed mortgage giants turbocharged the crisis.

The SEC's lawsuit shows that Fannie degraded its underwriting standards to increase its market share in subprime loans. The SEC also shows how Fannie led private lenders into the subprime market. In July 1999, Fannie and Countrywide Home Loans Company entered an alliance agreement that included a reduced documentation loan program called the Fast and Easy loan. Angelo Mozilo, Countrywide's founder, and Fannie were business partners in the subprime business. Countrywide found the customers while Fannie provided the taxpayer-backed capital. As Fannie expanded its subprime loan purchases and guarantees, the SEC alleges that executives hid investors' risk.

STUDENT LOAN MARKET

A similar situation occurs in the student loan market in which Americans owe over $1 trillion in student debt, which is more than total credit card debt. The government has set a goal for more Americans to graduate from college, encouraging an entire generation of Americans and parents who co-signed for their children, to mortgage their futures. The chances of their successfully paying off this debt are growing ever slimmer as tuition continues to increase, scholarships and grants are becoming scarcer, unemployment among the youth continues to increase, and a higher minimum wage eliminates many jobs. Current laws make it very difficult to erase student debt through bankruptcy.

COLLATERALIZED DEBT OBLIGATION

Because banks no longer keep mortgages and other loans in-house, an active secondary market has developed. When you borrow money, economists call the transaction between you and the bank the first market, and when the bank sells your loan to someone else, economists call this a secondary market. High-risk loans on the secondary market are called toxic waste. Investment banks could not compete with Fannie Mae and Freddie Mac in the mortgage market because Fan and Fred had the federal government's financial backing. Because of the Fed's guarantee, Fan and Fred could offer low return rates to investors and still attract customers.

How delightful would it be if these junk CDOs' sellers could receive the highest rating from Standard and Poor's and Moody's, the two major credit rating agencies? Now Joe Cassano and the AIG Financial Products Division enter the picture. By buying a credit default swap from AIG on a CDO, banks could argue that the CDO deserved a triple-A rating because AIG had a triple-A rating. When the mortgage market collapsed in 2007, and because AIG did not have the assets to support their massive credit default swap sales, the defaults caused a domino effect.

SECURITIZATION IS ALIVE AND WELL

So what is the current situation with securitizing debt into CDOs? As discussed above, the practice of securitizing debt is alive and well in the student loan market. Asset-Backed Securities (ABS) financed a large portion of the student loan boom in 2011. This practice resembles lending practices that overheated the housing market before the financial crisis. Banks and lenders relaxed standards to push more and more Americans into homes through subprime mortgages. Presently, some financial firms are packaging rental payments of residents living in previously foreclosed homes and selling these securities to investors, thus repeating the practices of subprime mortgages.

2008 FINANCIAL COLLAPSE AGAIN

When JP Morgan created the credit default swap (CDS) in 1994, the practice of swapping risk made good economic sense. So did the practice of securitizing debt into collateralized debt obligations. The fault was not in the process; the fault was in the fraudulent abuse of these practices. Since 2008 the government has criminalized mistakes, used poor judgment, and practiced ignorance, placing a burden on American businesses. The government punished minor errors with criminal charges and has attempted to regulate business activities through criminal law. Many business owners have accidentally broken vague and highly complex rules and have run afoul of the federal government.

WHAT DANGERS LURK AHEAD?

Years after the financial collapse of 2007-2008, we are still living in a reckless environment where the derivatives market is more significant than ever and is now in the hundreds of trillions. Speculators are still using excessive leverage while the national debt continues to grow. If we have a second crash, it could be worse than the first because we have spent so much on the first crash.

Repurchase Agreements (REPO) & ZIRP

The story of MF Global is an example of exotic and risky schemes encouraged by the government and the Federal Reserve because of the Fed's Zero Interest Rate Policy (ZIRP) and the downside of REPOs. A REPO is a repurchase agreement between two parties involving securities. A REPO is the sale of a security combined with an agreement to repurchase the same security at a higher price in the future. The party that initially bought the securities (reverse REPO) effectively acts as a lender. The original seller (REPO) effectively works as a borrower, using their security as collateral for a secured cash loan at a fixed interest rate.

The story of John Corzine and his company MF Global (MFG) has profound implications for the whole economy because it sets a precedence. MF Global bought Italian debt at a discount from Spain because Spain needed the money to prevent bank runs and maintain welfare programs. Spain agreed to buy back (repurchase) its Italian bonds from MF Global at a specified date in the future. MF Global gave Spain cash equal to the value of the Italian bonds minus a discount. Economists call the bonds that MF Global received reverse repos. At the same time, MFG records the sale as profit.

There is an inverse relationship between interest rates and bond prices. When interest rates increase, bond prices decrease and vice versa. If you had bonds for sale and interest rates in the market increase, how will you convince potential investors to buy your bonds? You have to reduce the price of your bond to attract buyers away from high-interest rate vehicles.

When Italy had to pay higher interest rates to promote its bonds, the price of MF Global's repos declined, forcing the Federal Reserve to issue a margin call on MF Global. Because MF Global did not have enough money to pay the Fed, Corzine took cash from customers' accounts, about $1.6 billion, to make good on the collateral call, bankrupting the company along with its client asset base.

Credit Default Swaps

Credit default swaps are alive and well today. Financial institutions such as JP Morgan Bank and Goldman Sachs sell credit default swaps offering protection from entire countries defaulting on their debt. For example, US banks and investment companies buy Spanish bonds. So, what happens if Spain defaults? Let's suppose that Citibank borrows money from the Federal Reserve at zero percent interest. Citibank then uses that money to buy Spanish bonds at six percent. Citibank then buys credit default swaps on Spanish debt from JP Morgan or Goldman Sachs, the two biggest sellers of CDSs. Citibank pays JPM or GS one percent or 100 basis points. In return, JPM/GS agrees to guarantee Citi's Spanish bonds in a Spanish default event. If a default occurs, JPM/GS will pay Citibank the money that Spain owed Citibank, and Citi would surrender the Spanish bonds to JPM/GS, who would keep the salvage value as well as any funds paid to them for the insurance. In essence, JPM/GS is writing insurance policies on the sovereign debt of whole countries!

ATTEMPTS TO LIMIT GOVERNMENT

There are no quick fixes to our problems, and no amount of creditism will grow the economy in the long-run, but there have been attempts. Senator Frank Church chaired the Church Committee in the 1970s to investigate abuses by the Central Intelligence Agency, the National Security Agency, the Federal Bureau of Investigation, and the Internal Revenue Service. The Committee found that the President or Congress had little authority; the deep state made up their own rules and did horrible things like assassinating foreign leaders, overthrowing governments, creating secret alliances, and spying on US citizens. Congress passed the first Foreign Intelligence Surveillance Act in 1978, designed never to allow rogue behavior without Congressional approval and executive consent.

President Ronald Reagan established the Grace Commission in 1984. For two years, 160 corporate executives and community leaders led an army of 2,000 volunteers to root out government waste—volunteer contributors with zero cost to the government-funded search. The Commission made 2,478 recommendations over 21,000 pages to cut costs without eliminating essential services to make the federal government more efficient and accountable to the taxpayer.

Congress passed the Gramm-Rudman-Hollings Act in 1985 as a follow-up to the Grace Commission, otherwise known as the Balanced Budget and Emergency Deficit Control Act. This act mandated the government live within its income and provided for automatic spending cuts to take effect if the president and Congress failed to reach established spending targets. The act gave the U.S. comptroller general authority to order spending cuts when necessary to meet spending goals. When the courts declared the law unconstitutional, Congress passed a revised version of the bill in 1987.

President Obama formed the Simpson-Bowles Commission, co-chaired by Erskine Bowles and Alan Simpson, to find remedies for the credit crisis of 2010. The Simpson-Bowles Commission recognizes that the ultimate solution to our economic problems is economic growth. Real, sustainable growth can only happen when society uses sufficient savings for productive investments. There is no easy fix to our concerns, and no amount of creditism will grow the economy in the long run.

The Commission outlined an ambitious package of spending cuts and tax increases and called for deep cuts in spending, a gradual rise in the federal gasoline tax, limiting popular tax breaks, and a child tax credit and the earned-income tax credit. It also called for an increase in the retirement age for Social Security, gave options for overhauling the tax system, cut Pentagon weapons programs, and reduced cost-of-living increases for all federal programs, including Social Security. Although more than 60 percent of Congress supported its recommendations, it never saw the light of day. The Twin Towers attack on 9-11 sealed our fate because it justified an aggressive foreign policy, including assassinations of foreign leaders, regime change wars, and unrestrained spending and debt.

CONCLUSION

The recession of 2007-2008 was arguably worse than any other recession since WWII, and it also ranks among the six or so worst America has experienced. Home foreclosures hit record levels as millions of people lost their jobs. Some economists call the period between 2007 and 2008 the Great Recession. If we were to pick a year the problems started, it would be 1995. In that year, Congress and President Clinton pushed for banks and other financial institutions to relax mortgage loan standards. Politicians wanted to increase mortgages, especially to low-income people. Mortgage lending institutions began relaxing standards for down payments, credit histories, etc. Many of the loans were considered subprime or Alt-A. Under pressure from Congress, Fannie Mae and Freddie Mac began pushing lenders to lend money to dubious credit history people. These easy lending standards led to the housing boom and the subsequent crash.

Late in 2004, the Federal Reserve began tightening credit, and by 2005, interest rates began to increase. The increased interest rates were problematic because many of the mortgage loans were variable, and thus the contracts pushed many borrowers into higher monthly payments. When many mortgagees could not make their monthly payments, they defaulted, thus bursting the bubble. Borrowers found themselves underwater with the housing market collapse, owing more on their house than what it was worth. People abandoned their houses and refused to make payments on their loans. By late 2007 consumer and business spending was down, and the economy slumped into a recession. When many people realized how worthless their MBSs, ABSs, and CDOs were, a worldwide financial panic ensued.

In 2008, the Federal Reserve acted to stem the tide of a financial meltdown. Before 2008, the Fed only lent funds to commercial banks and the federal government, but now it also lent hundreds of billions of dollars to nonbank corporations. Secondly, the Fed began purchasing obligations of Fannie Mae and Freddie Mac. Thirdly, the Fed agreed to exchange billions of dollars of risk-free federal bonds for billions of dollars of high-risk private bonds with commercial banks.

The economy faces two serious risks: the risk that higher taxes will drag on growth and the risk of continuing policies, such as the Dodd-Frank Law, that give bailouts and subsidies to specific industries. These actions will dampen productivity and economic growth by protecting inefficient producers and restricting resources' flow to the most productive users. The realization of these risks will lead to a permanent and growing decline in relative living standards.

The epic meltdown of 2007–2008 has caused changes in America. The breakdown has forced onto us two possible paths, leading to more government control and the other leading to a free market system. The winner of this great battle will determine our destiny far into the future.

ABOUT THE AUTHOR

I grew up in the golden age of rock'n'roll; the fifties was a decade when music changed from being parent-friendly to teenagers going wild over Elvis Presley, Chuck Berry, and Jerry Lee Lewis. I started college in 1963, the year the Beatles appeared on the Ed Sullivan Show. I remember lying in bed and listening to songs like "Let it Be," "Help," and "A Hard Day's Night."

Then there was that sobering moment sitting in the bleachers at Eastern Michigan University and hearing that Lee Harvey Oswald had assassinated John F. Kennedy. Looking back, I can see that events were taking us from traditions of baseball, apple pie, and family dinners together, to a world that has grown darker.

I was hired to teach economics at New River Community College in Dublin Virginia in 1972, which I am still doing. I have written four books before this one. This book was a struggle. I had to navigate through the propaganda, the disinformation, false teachings, half-truths, and groupthink of the mainline news media.

Made in the USA
Middletown, DE
24 August 2022

72027568R00139

John Maynard Keynes thought that the economy could tend toward less than full employment. In that case, the government must use fiscal policies to shift the equilibrium to a full-employment equilibrium. He believed that if we manage demand, we can manage the economy.

Friedrich Hayek believed that government cause long-lasting slumps. In his book *The Road to Serfdom*, he explains that government planning is the road to serfdom, the loss of personal freedom.

ROSE OF SHARON
PUBLISHERS

ISBN 9780996332729

FAMiLY-iD
intentional
Direction

Discover your family's unique purpose and passion.

To see each successive generation of
every family live more fully for God.

Greg Gunn

Foreword by
Craig Groeschel